Highlighted Readers' Review & Endorsement

"I truly appreciate the opportunity and would like to congratulate you on such a great and heartfelt work. The book is clear, engaging and easy to read, with powerful messages. I especially value how boldly and sometimes bluntly you challenge the reader's ego while offering a fresh perspective on leadership and human connection.

Your approach to interdependence is not just a theory, but a practical philosophy grounded in lived experience, which makes it both relatable and impactful. The logistics metaphors are also interesting and very effective.

It is an inspiring and thought-provoking book that reinforces a vital truth which I also believe the most: success without connection is empty, and interdependence is multiplied strength.

Congratulations and thank you for sharing it with me."

Turgut Erkeskin
President of Genel Transport
President of FIATA (2023-2025)

"In INTERDEPENDENCE – *The Language That Changes How We Live, Lead, and Love*, author, global connector, coach, and business leader Kristy Guo, in her latest book, offers more than a leadership message—she introduces a language for being human. The book positions interdependence not as an abstract ideal, but as a practical philosophy for life, leadership, family, faith, and global responsibility. At its core lies a simple yet confronting truth: 'We were never meant to live, lead, or succeed alone.'

Guo's perspective resonates with Isaac Newton's timeless observation that progress comes from 'standing on the shoulders of giants,' dismantling the myth of the self-made individual. Through lived experience, cross-cultural leadership insights, and deeply human stories, she shows how isolation diminishes both leadership and meaning, while connection restores purpose and resilience.

INTERDEPENDENCE challenges readers to rethink success—not as personal ascent, but as shared growth—reminding us that the future will not be shaped by the strongest individual, but by those who choose to lift others."

Professor **Issa S. Baluch**
Member of the Dean's Council - Havard Kennedy School (2017-2022)
Industry Lifetime Achievement Award Winner (2006, 2013, 2016)

"Thanks for sharing your book. It better allows others who may be struggling and becoming frustrated in reaching their goals of working with others. It offers a lot of insight into how to listen and work more effectively with others, locally or worldwide. Here are my thoughts on your book.

Interdependence is a book that has thought through how many people fall into a trap, thinking they are totally independent and do not realize how much we all depend on others to truly become independent in our own minds. The truth is that we need each other to some degree to truly become who we want to be.

Kristy has produced great thoughts and guidelines for almost everyone, as we all live and work with others. Add to that that many people work with others who are culturally different, and whose laws or customs are different, and they must be respected if you work in a global business world. By understanding and respecting cultural differences, you can easily achieve your goals. Not understanding that everyone thinks and acts as you do is a mistake that happens far too often. I feel this book helps you understand that to be independent you must be dependent on others in the world.

Reading this book may well help the reader understand that you must respect the culture and mindset of others who are also seeking independence, and that together you can really enjoy life and better achieve any goals you may have. You become dependent on others close to you, yet maintain your independence in creating a world environment that you truly enjoy.

Congratulations, Kristy, on putting together a true blueprint and a better understanding of your self-desire to achieve more, with the understanding that you need others to be interdependent and help you reach your personal goal of independence."

David Yokeum -*Chairman of WCA World*
(With over 9,400 member offices in 190 countries worldwide)

"INTERDEPENDENCE is a timely and thought-provoking book that challenges the myth of self-sufficiency and replaces it with a deeply practical philosophy for modern life. Rather than offering abstract theory, Kristy Guo translates big ideas into everyday actions—showing readers how connection, humility, and shared responsibility can reshape leadership, relationships, and personal purpose. With clear reflections, real-world examples, and tools readers can immediately apply, this book equips you to lead better, live more meaningfully, and build systems where everyone rises together. It's a compelling read for anyone who wants success without loneliness—and impact that actually lasts."

Dr. Steven Lim
Doctor of GP, Melbourne Australia

INTERDEPENDENCE

The Language That Changes How We Live, Lead, and Love

Kristy Guo

Copyright Disclaimer

Copyright © **2026** Cuilan Guo. All rights reserved.
This book, including all intellectual property rights therein, is solely owned by Cuilan Guo. No part of this book may be reproduced, distributed, or transmitted in any form or by any means, including photocopying, recording, or other electronic or mechanical methods, without the prior written permission of the copyright owner, except in the case of brief quotations for review, commentary, or other non-commercial purposes as allowed by law. Unauthorized use is strictly prohibited.

Publisher Disclaimer

This book is published by Signature Global Network PTY LTD. While the publisher facilitates the production, printing, and distribution of this book, all rights, ownership, and control over the content remain solely with Cuilan Guo. The publisher does not claim any ownership over the intellectual property contained within this book.

Accuracy Disclaimer

While every effort has been made to ensure the accuracy and completeness of the information in this book, the **author** and publisher make no representations or warranties, express or implied, about the accuracy, completeness, suitability, or availability of the content. Readers are advised to independently verify any information and consult with professionals where appropriate. The **author** and publisher disclaim any responsibility for errors, omissions, or any losses, damages, or disruptions arising from reliance on this book.

Similarity Disclaimer

This book is a non-fiction work and includes real-life experiences. However, names and details may have been altered to respect privacy and confidentiality, and any resemblance to persons, businesses, or incidents is coincidental unless otherwise noted with explicit consent.

Opinion Disclaimer

The views, thoughts, and opinions expressed in this book belong solely to the **author** and are not necessarily reflective of any affiliated organizations or entities. These opinions are based on personal experience and interpretation, and readers are encouraged to form their own views.

Explicit Content Disclaimer

This book may contain sensitive themes and discussions related to personal experiences, leadership, relationships, and human challenges. Reader discretion is advised. The content is intended for a mature audience.

Expertise Disclaimer

While the **author** has extensive expertise and experience in the fields discussed, this book is not intended to provide professional, legal, financial, or medical advice. It is meant for informational and educational purposes only and does not replace professional judgment. Readers should seek appropriate professional counsel for advice specific to their situation.

Publisher: Signature Global Network PTY LTD
Author: Cuilan Guo (Kristy)
Cover Design: Kristy Guo

ISBN: 978-1-7638198-7-0 (paperback)
ISBN: 978-1-7638198-8-7 (E-book)

Interdependence is the invisible language of life — when we lift others, we rise; when we isolate ourselves, we diminish our humanity, our leadership, and our future.

This is **not** a religious book, **not** a business book, and **not** a self-help book alone.

It is a **life philosophy + leadership manifesto + practical workbook** that explains:

- Why no human, leader, nation, or generation can thrive alone
- Why competition without compassion destroys long-term value
- How interdependence applies to **life, leadership, business, families, and global peace**

This book is written to serve audiences such as:

- Leaders, founders, CEOs
- Parents and families
- People questioning purpose, faith, humanity
- Anyone who feels successful yet lonely

What if the problems we are trying to solve — loneliness, broken leadership, divided communities, even war — all come from one forgotten truth?

Ready for the one truth?

We were never meant to live, lead, or succeed alone.

In a world that celebrates independence, competition, and personal success, *INTERDEPENDENCE* offers a radically different language — one that has quietly sustained families, communities, faith, and civilizations throughout history.

Through lived experiences, leadership lessons, faith-inspired reflections, and deeply human stories, Kristy Guo invites readers to rediscover what we instinctively know but often forget:

- You cannot be whole without others
- Leadership fails when humility is lost
- Wealth without connection feels empty
- Love multiplies when it is given away

This book is not about ideology. It is not about religion. It is not about business alone.

It is about **how humans thrive — together.**

Whether you are a leader, a parent, a builder of communities, or someone quietly searching for meaning, *INTERDEPENDENCE* will challenge how you see success, power, faith, and purpose.

Because the future is not decided by the strongest individual — **it is shaped by those who choose to lift others.**

Kristy Guo is a global business leader, community builder, and advocate for human-centered leadership.

As the founder of a global logistics and leadership network spanning more than 90 countries, Kristy has spent years working with CEOs, founders, and teams across cultures, industries, and belief systems. Her work has placed her at the intersection of business growth, leadership responsibility, cultural diversity, and human connection.

But *INTERDEPENDENCE* was not born from titles or achievements.

It was born from lived experience.

From building companies and communities across borders, to navigating leadership failures, cultural misunderstandings, loneliness at the top, and the quiet lessons of family life, Kristy has witnessed a universal truth repeat itself:

Whenever people rise by lifting others, systems heal.

Drawing from leadership practice, cross-cultural insight, faith-inspired values, and everyday human moments, Kristy writes not as a distant expert, but as a participant — someone still learning, still choosing, and still believing that love, humility, and responsibility are the foundations of a better future.

She believes the most important ideas are not the ones that impress — but the ones that transform how we live with one another.

INTERDEPENDENCE is her contribution to that transformation.

Acknowledgements

I am who I am today because of who I have met in life — those who have helped me, supported me, loved me, accompanied me, encouraged me, guided me, mentored me, educated me, failed me, fulfilled me, trusted me, and chose to be part of my life. You know who you are.

This book exists because of people. It is not just a collection of ideas or stories — it is the reflection of relationships, moments, lessons, and lives that intersected with mine. Every chapter carries fingerprints of those who walked beside me, challenged me, believed in me, and sometimes even hurt me — because all of it shaped who I am today.

To my beloved husband, **Luke**, and my precious daughters, **Sze Sze and Selena**:
You are my anchor, my home, and my greatest responsibility. Thank you for loving me through the chaos, for sharing both ordinary days and big dreams, and for giving me the freedom to fly while always reminding me where I belong.

To the **Signature Global Network family**:
You are not just part of a network — you are living proof of interdependence in action. Across cultures, borders, and beliefs, you showed me what unity with diversity truly looks like. This book carries your trust, your stories, and your courage.

To my dedicated **Signature team and staff**:
Your loyalty, resilience, and commitment turned vision into reality. You did not just execute tasks — you carried purpose. Thank you for leading with heart, integrity, and excellence even when the journey was demanding.

To you who ever shared your stories with me:
Thank you for your bravery in sharing your stories, your wisdom, and your lived experiences. This work reflects not just my voice, but a collective strength that deserves to be heard through the reflections of your stories too.

To my **C-suite coaching clients and global leaders**:
You trusted me with your challenges, your ambitions, and your doubts. Watching your growth, resilience, and transformation has been one of the greatest honours of my life. You constantly remind me why this work matters.

To my **church family**:
Your prayers, faith, and spiritual covering grounded me when the world felt loud. Thank you for reminding me that success without purpose is empty, and that love must always come first.

To my **friends, mentors, and supporters**:
You showed up — sometimes loudly, sometimes quietly, but always at the right time. Your belief in me, especially in moments when nothing was visible yet, became strength I could lean on.

This book is not mine alone.
It belongs to every leader, parent, dreamer, and change-maker who believes that life is richer when shared, that strength multiplies when we walk together, and that the world becomes better when we choose connection over isolation.

With all my heart,
Kristy Guo

Overview

Chapter 1 — *I Am Because We Are*

- Interdependence vs independence vs dependence
- Why loneliness is the silent pandemic
- Why happiness is impossible in isolation

A human alone survives; humans together thrive.

Chapter 2 — *Less Is More: The Mathematics of Life*

- Pizza, bakery, or seed
- Scarcity mindset vs multiplication mindset
- Why hoarding creates loss, and giving creates abundance

When I have less so others can have more, **the system grows — and I grow with it.**

Chapter 3 — *Interconnection: The Truth We Cannot Escape*

- Superstars need audiences
- Heroes are not heroes if they only save themselves
- Wealth, fame, success without connection is emptiness

If you don't understand interconnection, you don't fully understand life.

Chapter 4 — *The Leadership Paradox: Humility Wins*

- Why arrogant leaders fall
- Why humble leaders rise
- Your lived experience with fear-based leadership
- Asian / force-driven leadership vs human-centered leadership

Leadership is not power over people — it is responsibility *for* people.

Chapter 5 — Why Companies Win Together or Fail Alone

- Interdependence inside teams
- Silos vs unity
- Why culture beats strategy long-term

Interdependence turns competitors into ecosystems.

Chapter 6 — Love Your Enemy: A Living Lesson

- Doorbell story
- Forgiveness as strength, not weakness
- Children learning by example

Love is not passive. Love is courageous action.

Chapter 7 — We Are All Carrying Something

- Trauma, anger, sadness spill into others
- Why kindness must come before judgment
- Communities as families

We don't just fix houses. We heal people inside them.

Chapter 8 — Faith Over Fear

- Pain shakes faith, but abandoning faith deepens pain
- God's sacrifice reflecting interdependence
- Why belief systems shape civilizations

Faith is choosing meaning even when logic fails.

Chapter 9 — Purpose Is a Shared Responsibility

- Life is short, but legacy is long
- Saving lives, supporting others, choosing love

Purpose multiplies when shared.

Chapter 10 — The Global Language of Interdependence

- Why it transcends culture, race, religion
- Why it prevents wars and tragedies

Chapter 11 — Applying Interdependence to Your Life
Areas:

- Health
- Wealth
- Relationships
- Recreation
- Spirituality

Each section includes:

- Reflection questions
- Daily practices
- Interdependence scorecard

WORKBOOK & TOOLS
✔ **Interdependence Checklist**
✔ **Daily Interdependence Practice**
✔ **Reflection Questions**

Chapter 12 – Bonus – THE INTERDEPENDENCE FRAMEWORK™
*Interdependence in Action: The 3 Ls and the 5 Ps***

FINAL NOTE
This book is not meant to be read fast. It is meant to be **felt, lived, practiced, and passed on.**

Interdependence is not an idea. It is a responsibility. It is a choice. It is the future.

Contents

Invitation to the Reader

What you are holding is not a book about business, religion, or leadership alone.
It is about being human — and remembering what we were designed for.

It comes from lived experience, not theory.
From learning across cultures, building companies, failing, rebuilding, parenting, forgiving, and discovering that independence may create some success — but only interdependence creates meaning.
I have spent years working with leaders and teams across 90+ countries, navigating growth, conflict, culture, and connection.

The same truth repeated itself everywhere:
Whenever people rise by lifting others, systems heal.
Interdependence was not born from achievement.
It was born from loneliness at the top.
From cultural misunderstandings.
From broken leadership models.
From moments of humility, forgiveness, faith, and rebuilding.

This book is an invitation — not just to learn, but to practice.
To lead without domination.
To succeed without isolation.
To believe without superiority.
To love without keeping score.
I do not write as a distant expert, but as a participant — someone still learning, still choosing, still becoming.

May this book remind you of what the world forgets:
We are stronger because we choose one another.

K.G. — Interdependence begins here.

Foreword

Hi, my friend, this book is **a life philosophy + leadership manifesto + practical workbook** that explains:

- Why no human, leader, nation, or generation can thrive alone
- Why competition without compassion destroys long-term value
- How interdependence applies to life, leadership, business, families, and global peace

Danger Makes Us Isolate ourselves, but Connection Saves Us

When human beings sense danger, our first instinct is to pull back.

During COVID, countries shut borders.
Buildings closed.
People locked themselves indoors.

- Loneliness increased by **57% globally**.
- Depression rates **doubled**.
- Anxiety **tripled**.
- The WHO reported a **25% rise in mental health issues** linked directly to isolation.

Isolation was supposed to keep us safe.
But in many ways…
it broke us.

It made us disconnected from each other — not just physically, but mentally and emotionally.

I remember after three months of COVID lockdown, I was working in a global logistics company as the **Head of Trade,** managing my team in Sydney virtually. My mental health was challenged. I felt unfulfilled. I felt a bit depressed…

That was the time I became more intentional about reaching out to people, even long-distance, because deep inside me, I was telling myself — from my pride and ego — *"people need my encouragement."*

And then I realized **I needed them even more.**

The truth is — **we need each other.**

In my community, we became closer than ever.
We started regular weekly Zoom meetings.
We played bonding games through Zoom.
We cried and laughed together, even from behind screens.
We FaceTimed relatives we hadn't spoken to in years.

Suddenly, laughter was travelling through Wi-Fi cables.
The message was loud and clear:
Humans need connection more than we need certainty.
We survive **through** each other — not **away** from each other.

And no idea captures that more beautifully than the African philosophy of **Ubuntu:**

"I am because we are."
Or, **"I am a person through other people."**

I want to share **this story with you:**

> Sarah is talking to John — **a guy who talks to people daily because of his work needs.**
> Sarah: "So John, what is your dream one day **after you have finished working through your whole life?"**
> John: "To stay away from everyone, and **not need** to speak to anyone, and live my best life! I can just live in a farm and nobody can reach out to me!"
> Sarah: "What do you mean? But you're the guy who deals with people **every day**, and isn't that your passion?"

John: "Yes it is, **because I trained myself to, and I had to…**"

Sarah: "How about your family? Don't you want to bring them with you?"

John: "Oh yes, I will… **I have to.**"

Sarah: "You have to, **or you want to?**"

John: (**Pause**) "I have to and **I WANT TO.**

Sarah: "OK, but how about your family? Don't you want them to connect with others too? Your kids need friends."

John: "Yes, you are right, but… I just don't like chaos, and people cause chaos."

Sarah: "OK, I agree, John, but how about you? Are you perfectly behaved and **never annoying** people at any time?"

John: (**Paused again**) "No, I am not perfect."

Sarah: "Then why do you think others are annoying **just because** you want them to behave within your expectations? Tell me, John, are you happier when you are **by yourself** or when you are with someone?"

John: "… Well, I guess the **happiest** memories are with someone."

Sarah: "Exactly, John. Your problem is not to change others around you, but to change your philosophy and thinking. Do you always think others need you more and you are always the one who is **doing** or **giving**? What if others are thinking **the same**?"

This is just a made-up conversation, but I have to admit that **I have thought like John before**, and Sarah is the other version of me when I have this kind of self-conversation.

I believe we all have been there, because we all think that

we are independent, and we all want to look good, feel good, and be strong — **even if we are not, sometimes.**

Why is that? After reading this book, **you will find your own answer—the answer is in this book.**

As a high-performing coach, I've heard **enough struggles** from tired CEOs who love their teams and company staff, but ended up feeling weighted down. Some days there is a voice saying: **"Is it worth it? Why is it always me?"** You **will find your own answer through reflection after reading this book.**

Throughout my life journey is similar to everyone, it was:
Care less about others' thoughts (baby) →
Care more about others' thoughts (child) →
Care too much about others' thoughts (adult) →
Care less about others' thoughts (later adult life, after getting hurt and learning lessons) →
Care nothing about others' thoughts (aging, older)…
…but wait, do I really care no more about others' thoughts?

It is a lie. I can fool myself when I close my heart and ears and pretend nothing happened. But just because I close my ears and fool myself that everything is OK, it does not change the fact that someone just threw something in my face and hurt me — unless I run away, but in life, we have only one life and we live on one Earth. **How many times can you run away from trouble?** Even if you can, **how many times can you run away from people?** Even if you keep running away, **how many times can you completely forgive someone?** Even if you keep forgiving, **how many times can you let go of everything?**

I always love my favourite teacher Mr Jim Rohn's words: *"Don't wish it was easier, wish you were better."* The reflection of my saying: *"Don't wish others will change, wish you will change, change to be better and stronger."*

My friend, the good news is: once you become the master of **interdependence**, you will be better — because *99% of people* won't understand the dept of it and the benefit of it.

This is not a magic book. It is simply a book that will open up your mind, stimulate your new perspective, challenge your thoughts.

Don't read this book if you are not **open-minded** and **humble enough** to hear the different perspectives and the potential other side of you that you may constantly try to **bury or hide**. Because this book can be bold and blunt in a way that may hurt your ego.

But the good news is that if you are reading it and you decide to continue reading it, you are already 99% ahead of the game. The top performers, leaders and successful ones are always the small group, not the large group.

Who am I?

I was born as an illegal second child when there was China's one-child policy back in my time, and my very survival was based on **hidden networks**, but I founded a global network that covers members from more than **90 countries** after 4 years.

From suffering a difficult childhood to becoming talented in managing all kinds of relationships. From being a shy speaker to a confident world-class speaker, as well as running masterclasses for global CEOs. English is not my first language, but I've published *seven books in English* and more to come.

I wasn't born into a wealthy family. In fact, I was born in chaos and challenges.

I came from the humble beginning but got to live an abundant life with love, joy, wealth, health and success. The definition of success is that I get to dream big with passion, do what I love and help others to do the same. Life is a journey, not a destination, but so far my journey has been rewarding, and I believe yours will be too once you finish reading this book and apply what you reflected from it.

The reason I share this with you is because I want you to understand that if I started from being no one and having nothing, to where & who I am today — **so can you.**

Hang on a second -- I am not the most famous or richest man in the world, but I discovered my highest form of freedom and abundance, and I can confidently say that even if I have to restart from zero anytime and anywhere, I can still thrive with inner peace in depth.

It's not because I'm somehow special or more talented than anyone else. I genuinely believe that we are all equally gifted and have the same potential. The real difference between people comes down to the choices we make in life.

My life transformed only when my *perspective and philosophy* changed. If you'd discover the fast way to transform 90% of your life, and that is from your mindset, the 10% is a matter of step-by-step process, which is the easiest for anyone.

The purpose of this book is to equip you to create your own little handbook to live the best, most purposeful, and meaningful life — not just with abundance in wealth, but also with **healthy relationships**. As a leader, a parent, an influencer, an extraordinary person, you name it!

Interdependence is the answer

Experience & Evidence
Why me?
Growing up in poverty and constant struggle, being independent was always my go-to...

But my mindset shifted through direct conversations with global logistics CEOs across 190+ countries, connections with 30,000+ multinational leaders, and lessons from both their failures and my own.

As for me, after approximately forty years of my life experience (14,600 days), twenty-one-plus years of business experience (168,840+ hours), millions of dollars of failed deals from my mistakes. Winningdeals that produced billions for the companies I worked for, and achieved millions for the businesses I ran myself for four years. What I have reflected is this: If I had understood interdependence earlier, I could have done 10x, even 100x better.

Once you get interdependence right, you will be capable of making wise decisions in life.

As you and I both know — whether from a biblical or scientific perspective — our lives rely heavily on our choices.

The choice is YOURS.

The Honest Thoughts We All Have

Let's start with honesty. Have you ever said one or many of these?

"Oh, *people*... oh no, people! People are the problem!"

"Leave me alone, I just want my own space."

"I wish I didn't need to deal with people."

"People are so offensive — I can't say anything."

"People are annoying."

"People are selfish."

"I'm the most peaceful version of myself when nobody is around."

I know these thoughts well. I've had every single one.

But at the same time, I've had thoughts like:

"I wish someone could inspire me."

"It's nice to see families and friends together."

"I wish I wasn't alone."

That contradiction doesn't mean you are broken.

It means you are human.

Because relationships are not just life experiences — they are *human nature*.

If God created humans for relationship, if love is our highest priority, then connection is not optional — it's **foundational.**

The Truth Behind Those Thoughts

What we say to ourselves often feels true. But every thought has another side:

"People are the problem."
→ Yes. But people are also the solution.
"Leave me alone; I need space."
→ Space is healthy… until it becomes isolation.
"I wish I didn't have to deal with people."
→ Be careful — that belief quietly cancels opportunities, breakthroughs, support, and abundance.
"People are too defensive."
→ Sometimes they are. But so are we — when our ideas, boundaries, or advice are ignored. We judge others for the same behaviours we excuse in ourselves.
"People are selfish."
→ Yes. And sometimes selfishness is someone's attempt to survive. Just like sometimes being selfless becomes self-destruction.
"I am the most peaceful version of myself alone."
→ Of course. Because nobody is watching. No disagreements. No friction.

But without friction, wheels don't move.

Physics, Faith, and Reality

The Emotional Pattern — We All Live It
We think these reactions are random, but they aren't.
They follow a natural emotional sequence:

The Isolation Cycle
Hurt
→ Withdrawal
→ Protection
→ Loneliness
→ Craving Connection
→ Re-engagement

Nobody escapes this cycle — not CEOs, not parents, not leaders, not believers.

We're all learning how to be human with other humans.

Where PHYSICS Enters the Conversation

This is not just emotional or spiritual truth — it's scientific.

In physics, nothing exists alone.

Even the smallest parts of the universe refuse independence:

- **Protons need electrons** to form atoms
- **Magnets require polarity** — north and south
- **Light is defined by darkness**
- **Energy exists because of positive and negative charge**

A single electron by itself is just potential.

Only when it interacts does reality form.

Connection doesn't weaken existence — it creates it.

And just like electrons, humans are not designed to "be everything alone."

Even Einstein's theory of relativity teaches us something emotional:

Nothing has meaning by itself. Meaning comes from comparison, interaction, and relationship.

Success / failure.

Isolation / belonging.

Selfish / selfless.

Not opposites — coordinates.

So why can't we get rid of the negative?

Because **negative and positive charge is what creates energy.**

Darkness isn't the enemy of light — it is what makes light visible.

Resistance isn't the enemy of growth — it is what makes growth possible.

In life, in spirit, in physics:
Duality creates movement. Interdependence creates reality.
So yes, people can be annoying. So can we.
People can be selfish. So can we.
People can be disappointing. So can we.
But people are also where miracles come from.
Help comes from.
Healing comes from.
Breakthrough comes from.
We don't heal in isolation.
We heal in **interaction**.

Perspective

When people see a **half glass of water**, the argument tends to be this:

The **depressive and negative** people will say:

"It is a half glass empty, you cannot deny it."

But the problem is, they will not agree that *half glass full* is also the truth. Even if they know it, they will cover it and try to prove you wrong.

The **optimistic and positive** people will say:

"Come on, yes, it is half glass empty, but it is also half glass full."

They are not blind — they just choose a different perspective.

Because it is all about **your perspective**.

That is why I love Henry Ford's saying:

"Whether you think you can, or you think you can't — you are right."

From me: whether you think you are *half-glass empty* or *half-glass full* — **you are right**.

But what if the real question is:
Who are you drinking with?
Because a full glass means nothing…
if you have no one to share it with.

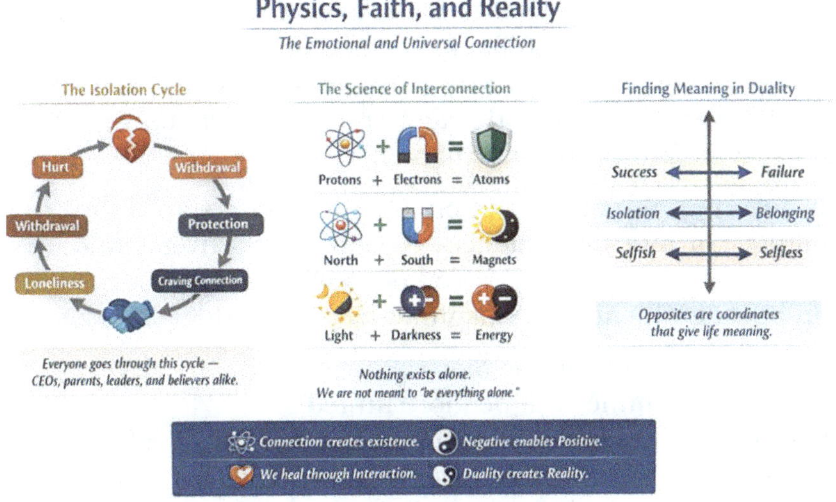

How to Make Full Use of This Book

Please do not just take notes on what I say, but take notes
on your reflections from what I say. You will discover the
most magical journey in any aspect of your life by mastering
interdependence.

At the end of it, all knowledge is yours, and I wish you tremen-
dous success! Because that is my purposeful life — to serve
you. And why? Because the ultimate beneficiaries will be both
of us! I am just being selfishly selfless. You've got this!

- **Leaders, founders, CEOs:** Use this as your handbook
  for your leadership approach and company culture.
- **Parents and families:** Use this as your family parenting guidebook, a self-check, and a way to create a new
  culture for your family space.

- **People questioning purpose, faith, humanity:** Use this book to reflect on your spiritual learning and practical lifestyle — your habits, your beliefs, your principles — and let it become an awesome humility-creating companion.
- **Anyone who feels successful yet lonely:** Use this to upgrade your relationship and lifestyle pattern.
- **Anyone who wants to have breakthroughs in life but feels stuck:** Use this to pause and reflect on your goals on your new chapter.

My hope is to see one day when everyone understands the language of **Interdependence** — when our children, children's children, grandchildren, and all descendants understand it and become fluent in it. Imagine what this world will become.

Leaders and CEOs will be more appreciated!
Parents and families will be more united!
No more suicides because people care and are cared for!
No more big fights because people understand that they are interconnected and interdependent.
No more selfish, silly decisions, because they understand that the ultimate party who feels miserable will be themselves.

It will become a big community with:
"I think for you, you think for me;
I serve you, you serve me;
I consider everyone, everyone considers me;
I love you, you love me;
Because it is always **us**, not I or you — always **us**!"

Chapter 1 — I Am Because We Are

UNDERSTANDING THE LANGUAGE OF INTERDEPENDENCE

African philosophy of **Ubuntu: "I am because we are." "I am a person through other people."**

"Ubuntu got his point but it doesn't apply for me, Kristy!" Maybe you will be thinking about this. Yes, I understand and I used to thinking that way too. Because I used to misunderstood the meaning of INTERDEPENDENCE.

Interdependence, Independence, and Dependence

"Kristy, I don't need interdependence. People need *me*. I'm independent. I'm strong."

I've heard this more times than I can count.

So let me gently ask: are we confusing *interdependence* with *dependence*?

Because they are not the same.

Independence means standing on your own feet. Dependence means you cannot stand without someone else holding you up. Interdependence is something entirely different.

Interdependence is when **strong, capable individuals choose to stand together.**

Not out of weakness — but out of wisdom.

Independence

in·de·pend·ence [ˌɪndɪˈpɛnd(ə)n(t)s]

independence (noun)
    the fact or state of being independent:
    "Argentina gained independence from Spain in 1816" "I've always valued my independence"
    Similar: self-government, self-rule, self-determination, sovereignty, self-sufficiency
    Opposite:
    Dependence, subservience

Dependence

de·pend·ence [dɪˈpɛnd(ə)n(t)s]
    noun
    dependence (noun)
    the state of relying on or being controlled by someone or something else:
    "Japan's dependence on imported oil"
    Similar: helplessness, weakness, defencelessness, vulnerability, subservience, subordination
    Opposite: independence,
    reliance on someone or something for financial support:
    "the dependence of our medical schools on grant funds"

Interdependence

inter·depend·ence [ˌɪntədɪˈpɛnd(ə)n(t)s]
    interdependence (noun)
    the dependence of two or more people or things on each other:
    "the new economic interdependence of the two nations"

    My interpretation of interdependence is simply this: ***Two or more independent individuals creates synergies, which means 1 + 1 = 3 or MORE.***

If you still believe Interdependent is being vulnerable or weak, it is not true.

Being interdependent is being intentionally to be strong TOGETHER!

The Hidden Cost of Disconnection

Why do we need to be clear about this language of interdependence? Because if we don't, it will cost huge problems.

Loneliness & Disconnection

Loneliness today affects:

- 1 in 3 adults
- 1 in 2 young people
- And the US Surgeon General says chronic loneliness is as harmful as smoking 15 cigarettes a day

Loneliness is no longer a private emotion — it is a global condition.

Across the world, adults feel isolated even while surrounded by people. Young people feel unseen despite being constantly "connected." Medical experts now warn that chronic loneliness damages our health as severely as longterm physical habits we already recognise as dangerous.

This is not a social inconvenience.

It is a human emergency! It is a global health emergency!

Logistics Metaphor

Let me explain this through the metaphor of logistics.

When connection breaks down in systems, the impact is immediate. In my professional world — logistics — even a single delay at a border can reduce trade and ripple through entire economies. One small blockage can cost billions. As logistics perspective, taking USA for example, one day delay could cause up to USD70 Billion per year if we based on the data of 2023.

*Economics research finds that **each additional day of delay in transporting goods is associated with around a 1 % reduction in trade flows** (trade volume or probability of exporting to a partner) when other factors are held constant. This is based on widely-cited work by Hummels and colleagues in the literature on "time as a trade barrier." From <u>Purdue e-Pubs+1</u>*

 *In other words: **saving one day of delay at a border (or conversely, imposing one extra day of delay) tends to change trade by roughly ~1%** relative to what it otherwise would be. <u>Purdue e-Pubs</u>*

📌 **Summary**

Metric	Estimate
U.S. annual total trade (goods & services)	*~ $7 trillion+ (2023) Resource from Wikipedia*
Impact of 1 extra day on trade volume	*~ 1 % reduction (academic literature) From Purdue e-Pubs*
Implied annual trade reduction	*~ $70 billion per year*

Human systems are no different.

When connection slows, breaks, or disappears, the cost shows up as anxiety, burnout, broken families, failed leadership, and empty success.

We Are Already Interconnected — Whether We Like It or Not

We often speak about connection as if it were optional.

It isn't.

Consider something ordinary you carry every day.

That object exists because strangers across continents worked in alignment — people who will never meet you, never know your name, yet contributed their skills, time, and effort so that object could exist in your hands.

Behind everyday convenience is a silent collaboration of cultures, labour, trust, and timing.

This is interdependence in action.

We can deny it. We can ignore it. But we cannot escape it.

If you are Gen Z, Gen Alpha, or any generation onwards — or if you have a child or grandchild from these younger generations — you will find that the **number one potential human crisis** is going to be a social connection problem. It is already happening everywhere with AI, which is so convenient, and it will only get worse as time goes by.

Even if people still meet each other sometimes, there is a huge sense of lacking trust due to the loss of deeper connection.

Imagine this: we no longer need to go out shopping for things — one click with our finger, and items can be delivered to your doorstep within 24 hours. In a future increasingly replaced by AI, the biggest problem will be mental health due to a lack of connection.

Companies are using robots, automation, and chatbots to communicate with each other.

Where are *you*?

What will *you* be doing?

One thing I am certain of: you will struggle to trust anyone, and you may not even be sure whether you are talking to a **real human** or just a robot.

Why this metaphor? Because **Global logistics** is more than moving packages — it's a universal language.

Every route, delay, and delivery reveals how deeply interconnected we are.

We must stop seeing **globalization** as a political debate and start learning it as **a language of interdependence.**

Take out your phone.

Hold it for a moment.

This is not a device.

It's a global love letter.

A collaboration.
A handshake between continents.

The minerals were mined in Africa.
Refined in China.
Designed in California.
Components engineered in Korea and Japan.
Assembled across Asia.
Moved by truck drivers, sailors, pilots, port workers, warehouse teams…

All so it could land in your hand— so you can text your mum, or scroll through social media.

That single device is more than a product — it's a *conversation*.

Millions of people across six continents "spoke" to each other through the shared language of logistics — a language made not of words, but of routes, codes, timing, and trust.

As far as I am not a fan of screen nowadays and my concern for the next generations for the extreme convenience and effectiveness of this device, it is still the proof of one truth:

We are interconnected whether we hide, isolate, or deny it.
Every time you hold this phone, you are holding the entire world.

Look at what you're wearing.

Pause for a few seconds.

Do you really believe it's all from the place you bought it?
It takes the whole world of teamwork to make that possible!
The cotton may come from Vietnam, the fabric from India, production from China, and the final label from Italy.

How about cars?

Take the Toyota Corolla — the world's best-selling car.
Its engine can come from Japan, the USA, and Germany.

Its transmission from Thailand and Japan.
Its tires from China, Malaysia, and Indonesia.

In short, *one Toyota Corolla can involve 25 to 30 countries* across its supply chain.

The average car has 30,000 parts — even if each supplier sources from just two countries, the web of involvement touches **over 60 nations.**

Too often, we treat globalization like a choice — something you opt in or out of.

That's like saying you don't believe in weather.

Whether you realize it or not, you're already speaking this language.

Every item you touch — your clothes, your coffee, your toothbrush — is a sentence in a story that crosses borders.

The real question isn't *if* you are part of the global conversation — it's *whether you understand what's being said,* and what role you are playing.

A one-day delay at a border causes a 1% drop in global trade, taking USA as an example, it will be about USD 5 billion dropping.

That's not just a statistic — that's a missed opportunity, a dropped signal, a broken sentence.

When low-income countries improve their logistics systems to middle-income levels, their trade rises by 15%.

That's what happens when more people are invited into the conversation.

Yet even as global e-commerce surpasses $6 trillion, most of us still operate with a local mindset — speaking only the dialects we know, unaware of the fluency all around us.

My friend, learning to speak *logistics* is like to speak *global,* means learning to understand the interconnection, and learning to *see the world completely.*

It means looking at your morning banana and realizing five countries collaborated to get it to your table.

It means understanding that when dock workers strike in Singapore, a small business in Seattle feels it.

It means rethinking "community" — not just as who you see around you, but who you rely on, and who relies on you.

The language of logistics is already shaping your life.

The question is: are you fluent?

Are you paying attention to the networks that sustain you?

Because when you do, everything changes.

You stop asking, "What's in it for me?" and start asking, "Who else is part of this?"

You stop seeing the world as divided and start seeing it as coordinated.

So tomorrow morning, when you pick up your phone or sip your coffee — pause.

Ask yourself: *What story did this item travel to reach me? Who made it possible?*

That's the beginning of fluency.

That's how we stop treating globalization as a debate — and start recognizing it as a language we were all born into.

Why Happiness Cannot Exist in Isolation

A human alone can survive.

But humans together thrive.

I learned this long before I had language for it.

When I was a child around 9-10 years old, my parents worked long factory shifts just to keep our family afloat. Many evenings, I was home alone.

I remember watching the clock.

Six o'clock passed. Six fifteen. Six thirty.

My stomach ached — but not only from hunger. I was hungry for safety. For belonging. For someone to come home.

There were no mobile phones then. I waited. I hoped.

Eventually, I stepped outside and sat near the gate as I said to myself: "Parents should be home, very soon… so that when they are home, I can immediately see them from the distance." I was watching neighbours return to warm kitchens filled with food, kid's laughter, and light. I felt hungry, not just my tummy, but my hunger for safety, love and family.

Then one of the neighbours near the door noticed me as she moved around the kitchen.

She seemed to see my desperation and hunger.

"Come eat with us."

I hesitated—my pride held me back for a moment—but then after pausing, I stepped inside.

And for the first time in a long time,

I felt connected again, I felt human again and I felt safe again.

That night I realized:
Sometimes the person who saves you does not have to be someone whom you know, they can be someone unexcepted from **your network.**

Interdependence is not about losing strength.
It is about **multiplying it.**
And once you understand this language, you begin to see life — leadership, success, love, and purpose — very differently.

Chapter 1 – I Am Because We Are

UNDERSTANDING THE LANGUAGE OF INTERDEPENDENCE

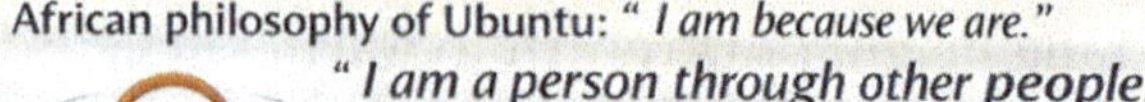

I am because we are."
" I am a person through other people."

The Interdependence Spectrum

Dependence	Independence	Interdependence
Relying on others to survive or function	Standing alone, self-sufficient. Strong alone.	Strong capable individuals choosing to stand together.
Fragile alone.		*Strong together.*

Interdependence **IS NOT Dependence** People confuse
this all the time.

The Hidden Cost of Disconnection

Loneliness & Disconnection

1 in 3 adults   **1 in 2 young people**

The US Surgeon General
*Chronic loneliness is
as harmful as smoking*
15 cigarettes a day

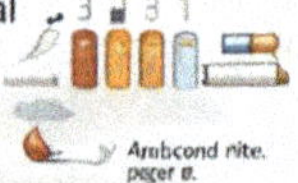

Human disconnection has real costs.

Proof of Our Interconnection

At a major border: 1-Day Delay = **$70 B**
Global Trade Loss

Proof of Our Interconnection

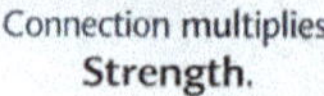

Connection multiplies
Strength.

Happiness and safety
Thrive in interaction

Interdependence =
Intentional collaboration
of strong individuals.

We are already interconnected whether we like it or not.

My Notes/Take-aways

Chapter 2 — Less Is More: The Mathematics of Interdependence

One of the biggest challenges we face in living an abundant life *with people* is fear.

The fear of not having enough.

The fear that someone might take what belongs to us.

This fear quietly lives inside many of us.

So when we meet new people, our first instinct is often not trust or openness.

It's more like:

"Wait a minute… will this person take something away from me?"

This fear is the opposite of interdependence.

Because interdependence begins with believing that **life is not a competition**.

The Bakery Lie

In real life—and especially in business—many people believe life works like a bakery.

If the bakery only makes **10 pizzas today**, once they're gone, they're gone.

If one person takes more, someone else gets less.

One wins.

One loses.

This is called a **scarcity mindset**.

But interdependence does not grow in bakeries.
It grows in **gardens**.
Before we continue, let me ask you:
What do you believe life is?
A bakery—or a garden?

A Cake, Three Children, and a Life Lesson

I once heard a story from **David**, a pastor and scientist.

One day, he shared the story that when he brought home a single slice of cake.

He had **three children**.
One slice.
Three kids.
You can imagine the tension.
Most parents would solve it quickly:

- "Give it to the youngest."
- Or "Cut it into three pieces so everyone stays quiet."

David did something different.
He placed the cake down and said:
"You three work it out."
Why?
Because, as he explained later:

1. **This is a family, not a restaurant.**
2. **They needed to learn how to solve problems together.**

They needed to learn sharing.
They needed to learn relationship.
They needed to learn interdependence.
Life constantly puts us in moments like this.
The real question is:
Do we protect, or do we participate?

God Did Not Create a Bakery

Thankfully, God did not create the world as a bakery.

In the Bible, it says God created a **garden**.
In a garden:

- Plants multiply
- Animals multiply
- Humans multiply

Everything grows.
Everything reproduces.
Everything starts with **seeds**.
You can count how many seeds are inside one pear.
But only God can count how many pears will grow from **one seed**.
That's because life is not a closed system.
It is an **ecosystem**.
And ecosystems run on interdependence.

Fact #1: The Law of Sowing and Reaping

I spent about **10 years** working in one company—from age **17 to 27**.

Think about that.
How many 10-year seasons do we really get in life?
When it was time for me to move on, I questioned myself:
"Did I use those years well?"
Looking back now, the answer is clear.
Because of that company:

- I travelled the world from age 18
- I met global CEOs across **190+ countries**
- I learned how real global business works

What did I give?
My time.
My youth.
My energy.
What did I receive?
Years later, I built my own **global network across 90+ countries**.

I now coach and mentor global logistics CEOs—many **20–30 years older** than me.

I was not highly paid back then.

But I was content.

Because I worked as if it were **my own company**.

I didn't officially start my business until four years ago, but I had been thinking like an entrepreneur for almost two decades.

Why?

Because interdependence works quietly.

When you genuinely contribute to others' lives, you don't lose—you **compound**.

If you want to reap, you must first sow.

Yet today, many people expect to reap without sowing.

Fast results.

Easy wins.

No effort.

But convenience destroys deep relationships.

When people don't invest, they later complain:

"Why am I not seeing results?"

Life is simply responding.

Fact #2: The Law of Average

What you consistently sow—on average—is what you receive.

In trust.

In health.

In business.

In relationships.

Interdependence is built through small, repeated actions.

Fact #3: The Law of Apple Seeds

You don't get apples by planting tomato seeds.

If you want respect, plant respect.

If you want trust, plant honesty.

If you want loyalty, plant loyalty.

If you want appreciation, plan gratification.
Life is fair—even when it feels slow.

Wanting more respect, check if you are planting respectful seeds to people around you.
Wanting more trust, check if you are planting trustful seeds (keeping your promises).
Wanting loyalty, check if you are planting loyalty to your relationships.
Wanting more appreciation, check if you are appreciating people around you.

What are fruits you want?
What seeds are you planting intentionally or unintentionally?

Fact #4: The Law of Unexpected Expectation

Sometimes, the unexpected outcome **is expected**.
You decide:

- How many seeds you plant

You do not decide:

- How many fruits will grow

That part belongs to life.
We live in a world obsessed with certainty.
But interdependence requires acceptance of one truth:

Life itself is uncertain.
Before I understood this, I wasted time chasing answers.
I felt lost when life moved fast.
Because if you are not careful:
While others are enjoying the fruit,
you are still studying the roots.

Fact #5: The Law of Good and Bad Seeds

Good seeds produce good fruit.

Bad seeds produce bad fruit.

Yet many people sow impatience, selfishness, or indifference — and expect kindness, loyalty, and trust.

Life doesn't work that way.

So the lesson is simple:

Be faithful to the good seeds you sow.

Let me show you what interdependence looks like in real life.

The Café Near Coles (The Story That Didn't End)

One day, Luke and I went to a café near Coles in our suburb.

I don't drink coffee—but Luke does.

The café is owned by a beautiful couple, around their 50s.

They were busy, yet warm and attentive.

They remembered Luke's order without him saying a word.

I thought:

"These people serve with heart."

I felt a strong desire to sow a good seed.

I said to the owner:

"This may sound a bit strange,

but I think you're amazing.

May I do something small to support you?"

He smiled, surprised and said OK.

"What's your name?"

"Sam," he replied.

I took a photo with him and Luke and shared it in our local community group, simply saying:

"Sam and his team are sweet and caring! He remembers your preference and always serves you with a big smile! Highly recommended."

I expected nothing. A few minutes later, already seeing 30 people liked and commented. Someone said "The best of the best."

"Sam is great same with his wife, she is lovely." Later 76 likes and hearts.

A few days later, Luke kept telling me:

"They're so grateful. They keep talking about it."

I did not expect that at all, but my heart felt warm and that fulfillment could never come from myself, but the appreciation from others, even though I did not expect any returns.

Two months later, we went back—this time to buy food from the café.

The lady – Sam's wife -- quietly leaned over and **gave my younger daughter a free donut.**

No announcement.

No expectation.

She said with an authentic smile to my little one Selena: "For you, little darling."

Me in a shocked face, paused for a few seconds, then responded: "Awww, you don't have to… Thank you. Selena, say thank you."

Selena, looking shy and said: "Thank you…"

We do not eat many sweets, it is not the thing that warmed us but her gesture that warmed us… and I had to accept to keep this eco system running.

The next visit?

Another surprise.

Later, near Christmas, we dropped off a small gift for them.

Not because we had to.

But because interdependence had been created.

No transaction.

No scorekeeping.

Just a relationship where **giving kept flowing both ways.**

That's how love lasts.

Fact #6: Everything You Do Is Planting Seeds

Words are seeds.

Actions are seeds.

Silence is also a seed.

Interdependence is always being built—or slowly broken.
What I've learned is simple:
Every relationship is a garden.

There is no such thing as a perfect **50/50** relationship.
Take marriage, for example.
Some days—most days—I'm not 100%.
Maybe I'm only **40%**.
On those days, Luke carries the other **60%**.
But sometimes, even when I'm only 40%, Luke may be at **20%**—not feeling well, exhausted, or overwhelmed.
And on those days, I still give my 40%.
Another time, I may be only **10%**, and Luke gives everything he has.
That's not imbalance.
That's **interdependence**.
We sacrifice for each other and this applies for all relationships.

A Small Parable: The Two Buckets

Imagine two people carrying water together.
Some days, one bucket is almost empty.
The other person carries more.
Other days, the roles switch.
But as long as **water keeps flowing**, the village survives.
The problem is not uneven buckets.
The problem is **empty intentions**.

One day, someone saw Luke doing most of the housework.
A friend—who didn't really know us—said to him:
"So she doesn't need to do anything?"
Luke was shocked.
Then he laughed and replied:
"No. We're a great team."

Why does this rule work?
Because when the fruit hasn't grown yet,

we intentionally **plant more seeds**.

We always keep the emotional bank **in credit**.

Words matter.

Luke's love language is appreciation, so I speak it often.

Actions matter.

I cook dinners, bring fun into the home, create games, laughter, and connection.

Luke does the laundry, the gardening, school drop-offs, and pick-ups—often more than I do.

It's not about who does more.

It's about **why we do it**.

The goal is shared: a flourishing relationship, unity, and love that lasts.

We are both independent people.

But when we come together—

1 + 1 doesn't equal 2.

It equals 3… 4… and more.

I call it the **synergy of independence – interdependence!**

Fact #7: The Law of Proactivity

Seeds do not plant themselves.

Someone must plant them.

And that someone is **you**.

Waiting for others to invest in you is like waiting for someone else to live your life.

Every meaningful relationship in my life—business or personal—started because **I moved first**.

Almost every entrepreneur I coach tells me the same story:

"My first client came because I reached out."

Many of those clients stayed **10–20 years**.

Interdependence rewards those who initiate.

A Short Parable: Two Doors

Imagine two people standing in front of two closed doors.

Both are waiting for the other to knock.

Nothing happens.

But the moment **one person knocks**, both doors open.

I've never seen a relationship flourish when both sides wait.

And I've never seen a relationship fail when both sides are willing to move.

In my life—as a leader, a spouse, and a mother—I noticed something very clearly:

When I wait for something to happen, knowing that I can start or move first, I suffer.

First, my time is wasted.

Second, silence creates misunderstanding.

Third, I lost the control of that time.

About **90% of people assume negative meaning from silence** — even when none exists.

That's why most gatherings, connections, and reunions in my life are initiated by me.

Being proactive gives you **authority over your time**.

As an entrepreneur, you don't want others managing your time—or taking your opportunities.

You want to be the **director of your own life**, not an extra in someone else's movie.

The good news?

Proactivity gives you control, clarity, and peace.

A successful life—and every successful relationship—begins with the law of proactivity.

Fact #8: The Law of Multiplication

Scarcity mindset says:

"If you win, I lose."

Interdependence says:

"If we grow together, we both win."

Only one creates a future.

A company that understands multiplication builds a culture of **unity**.

A leader who understands multiplication leads with **wisdom**.

A parent who understands multiplication raises children with **confidence and charm**.

A person who understands multiplication creates **leveraged wealth**—not just money, but people, trust, and opportunity.

A team that understands multiplication becomes a **self-motivated A-Team**.

A child who understands multiplication grows up strong— not afraid to share, not afraid to lead.

A Short Parable: The Candle Room

One candle lights another.
The first candle doesn't lose its flame.
The room simply becomes brighter.
That's multiplication.

Fact #9: The Law of Receiving

Hoarding creates loss.
Giving creates abundance.
When I choose to have a little less
so others can have more—
the system grows.
And when the system grows,
I grow with it.

One day, our family of four were walking on the streets of the Melbourne CBD. Suddenly, my two kids spotted a homeless man. They both looked at me, and I knew what they were thinking—because I was thinking the same thing.

So I gave them both coins and cash. They went and put the money into his can, then left with joy.

The old man, who looked around 60, with a messy appearance, looked deeply grateful and responded immediately, "Thank you!"

That night, when I was taking my older 11-year-old daughter, Sze Sze, to bed, I wanted to use this story to help her understand what the Law of Receiving really means. So here was our conversation:

Me: "Sze Sze, remember today when we gave money to that homeless guy?"
Sze Sze: "Yes."
Me: "How do you feel?"
Sze Sze: "I feel sorry for that guy. I feel happy after giving."
Me: "That is great. Do you think when we give, who gets more—the giver or the receiver?"
Sze Sze: "Of course the receiver… but wait…"
(thinking with her smart little mind, wondering that Mum wouldn't ask if the answer were so obvious)
So she continued:
Sze Sze: "Both?"
Me: "Yes—but no. I believe it is always the *giver.*"
Sze Sze: "Why?"
Me: "Because yes, the receiver feels happy and can keep what they receive for a while. But for us, the ones who give, this story will be remembered forever—and the sense of fulfillment will last forever."
Sze Sze: "Ohhh… that makes sense. And that is true."

Here you go—when you start giving, **receiving becomes automatic**.

A Final Parable: The Open Hands
Closed hands can't receive anything new.
Open hands may look empty for a moment—
but they are the only ones that can be filled.

Less is not loss.
Less is leverage.
Less is love in motion.
This is the mathematics of INTERDEPENDENCE.

Chapter 2 – Less Is More:
The Mathematics of **Interdependence**

My Notes/Take-aways

Chapter 3 — Interconnection: The Truth We Cannot Escape

There is a truth about life that no one can escape — whether you are rich or poor, famous or unknown, young or old.

That truth is **interconnection**.

Think about it.

- Superstars need audiences
- Leaders need followers
- Teachers need students
- Parents need children
- Heroes are not heroes if they only save themselves

Even the strongest person in the world still needs **someone**.

If you don't understand interconnection, you don't fully understand life.

Success Without Connection Is Empty

You can have:

- Money
- Power
- Titles
- Achievements
- Fame

But without connection, all of it feels strangely hollow.

I've met incredibly successful people—people with global businesses, awards, and influence.

Yet behind closed doors, some of them feel deeply lonely.

Because success without interconnection does not satisfy the human soul.

Aristotle said it clearly more than 2,000 years ago:

"Man is by nature a social animal."

In other words, we are wired for connection.

You cannot be truly happy in isolation.

Loneliness is not the absence of people.

Loneliness is the absence of **meaningful interdependence**.

Superstars and the Illusion of Standing Alone

Let's talk about superstars.

A singer without an audience is just someone singing alone in a room.

A speaker without listeners is just someone talking to themselves.

Michael Jackson—one of the greatest performers in history—once said that the energy of the audience gave him life on stage. Without them, the performance meant nothing.

Superstars don't shine *because* they are alone.

They shine because millions of people are connected to them.

The same applies to leaders.

A leader without followers is not a leader—just a person with opinions.

Leadership itself is proof of interconnection.

Heroes Are Not Made To Save Themselves

A hero is only a hero because someone else is saved.

If a firefighter runs into a burning building and saves no one, there is no story.

If a business leader builds wealth but lifts no one else, history doesn't remember them kindly.

Mother Teresa once said:

"If you can't feed a hundred people, then feed just one."

Her life reminds us that meaning is not found in how high we climb alone, but in how many people we lift with us.

My Own Journey With Interconnection

I did not build a global logistics network across 90+ countries by myself.

That would be impossible.

Every country represents:

- A trusted partner
- A relationship built over time
- Mutual value exchanged
- Interdependence in action
- My team members who are in this journey with me together

When I started, I didn't have power or scale.

I remember having to completely humble myself every single day, in every moment, so that I could reach out to people—asking for recommendations, support, and advice from those who already had experience. My first ten founding members mostly came from my previous connections and networking experience. Some of them were connected with me through social media and had been observing my journey from a distance.

I worked extremely hard to make calls and set appointments with potential connections. Sometimes they were the right fit. Sometimes they weren't—but they would introduce someone else to me instead.

Along the way, I was rejected many times.

I felt overwhelmed dealing with IT setup.

I lost some of my joy because the pressure was too heavy while I was still a startup.

I had no direct mentors, no financial support, and no existing clients at all.

I had to start completely from scratch.

What I had was willingness—to show up, to contribute, to connect.

Over time, people opened doors for me.
Not because I demanded access,
but because connection created trust.
And trust created growth.

Why Money Alone Never Feels Like Enough

Viktor Frankl, a Holocaust survivor and psychiatrist, wrote in *Man's Search for Meaning* that humans can endure almost any suffering—
as long as life has **meaning**.

Meaning does not come from money.

Meaning comes from:

- Being needed
- Being useful
- Being connected

This is why some retirees feel lost after leaving work.
This is why some wealthy people still feel empty.
Because interconnection is not optional.
It is essential.

Do not get me wrong, my misunderstanding about money caused a lot of pain to my family and my initial part of life. Money itself is NEVER the root of evil. It is the best thing you can have. But it is NEVER the answer to solve all your problems. It will only create evil if you believe that it can solve all your problems.

Simple example, you received 10 million dollars today but did not create any impact or help to anyone in your life, and the money will only stay at your bank account, compared to you receiving one skill to earn one million dollars today and more in the future, and the skill you have can immediately help millions of people and can be taught to your next generations, and creates a legacy that will last. Which one will you choose?

I know it sounds extreme, but it is happening every day. When we focus on chasing money, we get to stuck at the 10M cash focused intention, and it is not going to take us further or last for a while. But if we focus on creating value for PEOPLE around us, there will never be a roof, because sky will be your limit!

Why Purpose Matters

The true growth comes from the day when you understand WHY when you do anything. You can copy others, you can follow what others are doing and never ask questions, but the day when you are doing something and knowing deeply about the WHY behind it is the day you truly understand your life meaning – purpose.

One of the most influential speakers in leadership topic – Simon Sinek has his famous TED talk and leadership book called <<Start with Why>> It is so influential that many companies use his method and it completely changed the game.

I always share this concept with my CEO friends – Find out your WHY, your what, who and how will come along the way automatically. This is the reflection of the famous bible verse "Where there is no vision, the people perish." — Proverbs 29:18. A life living without purpose is not a life worth living. I believe a person lives on earth that never find his purpose is not different than a robot. We are mean to live a purposeful life.

If you find yourself losing passion and joy, there is only one answer – you lost your purpose. Maybe the whole life you have been chasing for a lot of things, but you may not find out that everything you are chasing is simply related to PURPOSE. The secret of success, happiness, joy all comes down to living your life with purpose.

If you have been a parent and you lost your passion, ask yourself why you do what you do… soon you will find your joy back once it is aligned with your WHY. Is it because you want to create a dream family? Is it because you want to leave a legacy that your next generations will have better lives and better stories to tell? Be honest with yourself. These are understandable points.

If you have been a CEO, Entrepreneur and you lost your passion, ask yourself why you start your business from day one, and what is the final purpose behind all of these… soon you will find your true vision and answer that will ignite again your passion. Is it because you want to live a better life, with financial and time freedom? Is it because you want to leave a great legacy? You want to create a successful business that will last and will bring you more fulfillment and freedom? Embrace these reasons, because they will give you power. You will only get stuck when you say to yourself: "Not really, I just need to have enough. I am content."

Why? Because if your purpose is so big but you sugarcoating it to be smaller just because you are worried about how others are going to judge you, you will never find the true freedom. Truth can set you free!

Be bold to explore your why – your purpose, dream big and declare it! Write down 100 reasons of why you want to achieve those goals, because there is a superpower behind the word – WHY.

All high-achievers know their WHYs, and they carry them DAILY!

Now it is your turn!

Just remember – your purpose must be aligned with INTERCONNECTION and INTERDEPENDENCE. If your WHY is simply about your person desire and greed, sorry but not sorry to say: you will never be fulfilled.

Chapter 3 — Interconnection: The Truth We Cannot Escape

Fulfillment and meaning come from finding and living your WHY.

My Notes/Take-aways

Chapter 4 — The Leadership Paradox: Humility Wins

How does interdependence get something to do with leadership?

What was your belief about leadership? Coming from an Asian background, leadership tends to reflect as "power" and "authority". That is why in most Asian cultures, the leaders are simply the bosses. You do not need much to be a leader. Money, authority and frame, and you may just get a leadership role.

However, just because you wear an eagle badge doesn't make the little duck an eagle. Just because you have power doesn't mean you are a true leader.

Leadership is not about power over people — it is **responsibility for people**. True leadership requires humility, courage, and the integration of **truth with love and grace**.

One joke but a true story is what we always laugh about.

Mr Chan opens his company, and so when he starts to answer the phone calls, he becomes Security Guard Chan, little Documentary Clerk Chan, Customer Service Chan and Toilet Cleaner Chan.

It sounds funny but it is true that if you only have yourself playing the solo role or multiple roles in life without others involved, you are technically not a leader. A leader has his followers. A leader influences, empowers and transforms lives. A one player game is dull.

I want to share a vivid anecdote from my very early leadership days in the corporate world:

Leading a team as a new manager in logistics at an age of 19, initially relying on strict, fear-based control. Back then I was new and I had to perform well to show that I am qualified to my role, so I decided to go 100% powerful and responsible. I had to do what others are doing.

At the beginning, I didn't understand about leadership. From what I have learned from earlier days as I did not have a specific mentor, I just followed my instinct to use manager as power. I micromanaged everyone's time-in and time-out. I forced them to use my way to do everything.

It worked a bit, and team came to work in time, but something wasn't right afterwards, employees compiled, but I found the results were surface-level, innovation was stifled, and trust was fragile…

There was the time sitting in the office felt like in a prison. Deep inside of me knowing this raises the red flag but because I am fearful of losing my manager title, I still went with the flow.

One day one of the team members Lancy came to me and submitted her resignation letter. Strangely, that hurt my feeling as I always loved Lancy and treated her extremely special, little did I know I was still new to the leadership game. That was the biggest lesson ever, and I knew this had to change.

Thanks to that experience. I decided to be the different one. From that day, I started to lead the way how I wanted to be treated. Using the principles of treating others as how you want to be treated, I managed to make a lot of hard decisions that includes taking full responsibility of mistakes the team make and giving credit to them even when I supported them to achieve anything.

Not only I did that to my team, but also I did that to the whole community. Other managers and anyone who works with me. That completely transformed my life. Not only I became one of the most favourite leaders to the company staff, but our team members are also proud of being in the department and many are dreaming of getting a role in our department.

I only did one thing, prioritizing humility over power, and the power of humility is more powerful than the power we know.

What I learned?
The fear-driven environment produced efficiency but no loyalty.
Coming from the Asian force-driven background to go to the narrow-road of human-centred leadership gate isn't easy but it is defi-nitely worth it.

Asian / Force-Driven vs Human-Centered Leadership

- Force-driven approach emphasizes obedience and hierarchy.
- Human-centered approach: respect, coaching, empowerment.

What's even better, during the time I led in the company, the company culture started to be influenced by the way how I led, it had made a huge contribution to the success of the company where I used to work with. In less than 10 years, the company started with 50 staff to 4000 people and became the billion-worth company with a healthy culture.

Fast forward to 11 years ago at the last month before I offi-cially resigned from my position as I needed to immigrate to

Australia, our managing director Victor arranged a huge farewell party for me. We went to a huge dinner and karaoke.

All my 20+ team members came and all other department head, senior managers and even team from other departments with total 50+ people, pushed away all events and came to my party. Surprisingly, at the same time, I also got almost everyone in Hong Kong office where I stayed 1/3 of time farewelled me the next few days. I felt special, touched and highly appreciated.

I still remember the day when my Managing Director dropped me off and said goodbye to me after the massive farewell party, (I mentioned part of this to my book The World's Thought Leaders, here is the whole conversation) he said to me: "Kristy, you are indeed someone! I've never seen a person who is so influential – the fact that when you were singing and asked them to dance and they all moved in unity and beautifully…" Me, paused and then smiled back with huge gratification: "Thank you!" That boosted me so much to the inner identity of me who is saying to myself: "Hey, you are indeed someone! You are born to be a leader…"

The fact that I am telling all these stories proudly is a live proof that the success I built on leadership journey is reflected in the way how they respected me and appreciated me as well. I am carrying these stories until today, and they still fill me with confidence, joy and passion!

It is never just me or just them. We are all interconnected and that is the power of interdependence.

Do you have the similar stories? When was the last time you felt that sense of achievement and fulfillment? When was the last time you heard something people praise about your efforts, influence and the difference you have made?

Let that sink in and let yourself enjoy that sense of

self-esteem, pride and fulfilment, which is needed and highly recommended.

Now, let it go deeper, let your humility come to play. Ask yourself: is it true that without these people appearing in your life, without their presence, you couldn't do what you do, the story will be different? Is it true that it is always the interconnection and interdependence that reflects the true power?

Here are what I believe about humility:

Humility is not lessening yourself, it is thinking for others more! With the law of interdependence, when you think for others more, all rewards will come back to you automatically. I do not know why but the rule just works. There is not anyone who is crowned to be worshiped or loved if that person only thinks for himself. All heroes are those who think for others first. You can choose to be a hero or a zero by choosing humility or arrogance, and it is not a rocket science.

Humility starts with human and ends with ability. It is an acknowledgement of being a human not to be perfect, but to be real.

The real wisdom comes from knowing we know nothing and there's always something we can learn from others.

Jesus is the humblest character in bible yet the highest king that everyone worships. He serves and washes his disciples feet while he is also the might king. If you are doubting to have both exist at the same is possible, his story proves that they are co-existing, they are interconnected- meaning if you want to have the crown, you also need to have the humility and the heart to serve others.

A true leader does not need a badge or crown but he always wears an invisible crown of humility.

Love + Truth + Grace Framework

Here is a framework I use to lead my team no matter who I lead and where I go:

Love + Truth + Grace Framework

Core principle: *Truth without love and grace won't transform souls; love without truth is not true love.*

During my coaching program, some global CEOs who are truly struggling with leadership. I want to share one of the conversation I had with one of my CEO mentorship clients, to protect the privacy, will change the name of him, let's call him Johnny.

Johnny is a charismatic leader, and he owns a company that runs 8 figure yearly and 5 offices with hundreds of staff.

Now he is with me at the mentorship session. He looked super heavy, frustrated and burdened.

Me: "Hey Johnny, so is there anything you are struggling the most that I can help?"

Johnny: "I am p*ssed off by one of my long-term working employees -- he is making drama. He is the problem because he has problem with everyone at the moment. I may have to get rid of him if I cannot change his behaviour, as it becomes toxic to all other staff and it is going to affect the business too."

Me: "Oh, sorry to hear about this situation, Johnny. How long has this person been in the company?"

Johnny: "Well, quite a while now, since he was the staff who joined us quite early."

Me: "So have you had an honest conversation with him?"

Johnny: "Yes, I did… I was very angry at him."

Me: Paused… (It looks like it is spreading lots of fear, so I assume the situation will not be improved, but will be worse, because the whole reason why this person makes drama is he is feeling insure about his job… he has to prove a lot of himself or beat others down to keep himself safe.)

"Johnny, do you still need this person in the company? Does he contribute to the company?"

Johnny: "Yes, I believe so, but if he cannot change, I'd rather not to keep him, not as I want to but for the sake of the company's growth."

Me: "Ok, Johnny, have you tried to have a conversation with him to ask if he is OK and with more care and love?"

Johnny: "No… I was very mad at him."

Me: "Look, you got nothing to lose Johnny. Here is what I believe. I believe you are an amazing leader, you love your team, you love your company. You work tirelessly to fight for more so all staff can get paid more and live better lives. Agree?"

Johnny: "Yes."

Me: "Your goal is to achieve a win-win outcome. When was the last time you had a one-on-one conversation with your main staff, your direct reporting lines?"

Johnny: "Don't remember, maybe 3 months ago… no fixed time."

Me: "This is what I want you to do. In order to save your time, make your time more worthwhile and to stay on track with your core members, I need you to schedule the fixe time to meet them for one-on-one at least once a month. More casual conversations to understand how they are doing in a personal level. Because first, they may have some personal things going on in life; second, everyone needs a mentor and you are their mentor. You are the head and they are the body, when body cannot receive the regular signal or instructions from the head, they panic, they get lost…"

Johnny: "Sound good. How do I do it? I hate these kinds of conversations."

Me: "Use the Love + Truth + Grace Framework. You can also call it Sandwich conversation which someone else calls it but I have an upgraded version you just need to follow it."

Johnny: "Sure, tell me…"

Me: "So you start your conversation with love and care and starting with praise and appreciation. You say things like: 'Hey xx, I want to acknowledge your efforts and loyalty to this company, and thank you so much for being amazing at xxx another day.' Be specific, be genuine and sincere. You know that person, you can definitely find something to praise him about.

"Then you affirm his identity, I would say – 'Hey xx, you know how important you are to me and the company,' so he drops down his defence and feels safe to be with you to this conversation."

Johnny: "Ok, that sounds good…"

Me: "The second step – **Truth**. This is the hardest step, because almost everyone hates the hard conversations, but the hard conversations are the most meaningful and important conversations that we need to have. As long as you master these kind of conversations, it transforms your life and business. A hard conversation can avoid dramatic tragedy, it avoids misunderstandings and violence."

Johnny: "Yes, I definitely avoided these conversations as much as I could before…"

Me: "Johnny, you are a high-achiever, and this is the best time to act as your true character and leadership charisma. So before you start talking about the truth, I need you to PRIME him first. Priming will help to first give him a signal so he is not going to be shocked. Imagine you start a sandwich conversation just like taking him the roller coaster, he can get madder and if he has heart-disease, he might get a heart-attack because of the contrast…"

Johnny laughed loudly: "Haha, so true!"

Me: "I need you to say something like – 'Hey, no matter what we are going to discuss today, I want you to know that this is not personal. I want to discuss with you for something how we can improve together so we can achieve the same goals, OK?' Then he should definitely say yes. You can then add: 'Can we talk something seriously now, if it is a good time to talk about it?' If you want to mention a specific incident, you can mention a bit now so he has time to prepare his mind and heart."

Johnny: "That sounds interesting." He started to write down all the notes while listening.

Me: "Then you can start telling him your concern about his recent behaviour, but you start with 'Are you ok XX? The reason why I am asking is because I have seen some behaviours that are badly affecting the company culture. I know it is not your intention so I want to understand the stories behind it.' Then let him talk… Once he finishes talking, you acknowledge and thank him, and ask him what he thinks about the solution and pause, to give him time to have critical thinking. Remember people will only do things when they believe that decision is made by themselves, nobody wants to be told what to do. The golden rule, never direct any mistake to their identity. When talking about mistakes, always direct it to the thing, not the person (identity)."

Johnny: "I like that approach." (continues to take notes.)

Me: "I am glad. This works, Johnny. Now he may bring up some plans of the solutions, you just need to listen, then you can use the last layer and say to him things like 'thank you for being honest, being part of the huge success of the company. I believe our goals are the same, and I believe you know what to do to improve this. I trust you! If you need any support, I am always here.' To say this will help to boost his leadership skill confidence and guide him to be more determined to make the change himself."

At the end of the coaching session, I asked Johnny, "How do you feel now?"

Johnny: "I definitely feel much lighter... thank you."

2 weeks later, Johnny came back to the mentor session and thanked me a big time. "Kristy, it worked so well. I sorted out all my core members problem. Now when I'm away, I don't get many calls or messages anymore, and my team is more independent and confident to deal with more things."

Me: "That's awesome! How about that guy you had trouble with?"

Johnny: "He appreciated me so much and he has changed a lot with his behaviours, and he apologized as he was worried about losing his job... it's all good now, thank you!"

Remember: ***Love + Truth + Grace*** *Sandwich* This framework transformed team dynamics, retention, and long-term loyalty.

"Leadership is not the ability to command — it's the ability to lift people. Humility doesn't weaken you; it makes you invincible."

Johnny didn't just become a better leader by changing his perspective and approach. He becomes happier, lighter, and joyful again. Because the fact that you may want to be absent from your leadership role won't help you, but the fact that when you understand that every conversation and every role is an opportunity of interdependence and not only the person you need to deal with needs you to deal with him, but also you need to deal with, because at the other side of this pain, there is the light at the end of the tunnel that transforms you and equips you to be stronger, better and wiser for any bigger challenges in life. Every challenge is an opportunity! How amazing is that!

Chapter 4 — The Leadership Paradox:
Humility Wins

My Notes/Take-aways

Chapter 5 — Why Companies Win Together or Fail Alone

Interdependence turns competitors into ecosystems.

And long before strategy fails or systems break, a company either rises or collapses based on one thing: **whether its people can stand together.**

The Illusion of Winning Alone

For years, the business world celebrated the idea of the lone winner.

The heroic founder.

The dominant company.

The smartest individual in the room.

But reality tells a quieter, truer story.

Even the most brilliant individuals fail when they are surrounded by disconnected teams.

Even the strongest companies weaken when departments protect themselves instead of supporting one another.

No organization collapses overnight.

It fragments first.

With the new generations coming on-board as we heading to GEN Beta, more and more global CEOs will be struggling to find fitter and better candidates to work for them. One of the hardest truths they are not aware of is the mindset that to run a business is no longer just a number game or sales game, it is more a people game and a leadership game. More attractive leaders will get better talents, as newer generations are no longer just working for money as they are not as desperate as their parents' generations.

It is always a 'we' and 'us' game, not a spotlight on 'you' or 'me' game.

Why Signature Global Network Exists

Signature Global Network (SGN) was never created to be "another network."

It was born from a very real pain I saw repeatedly in the logistics industry:

Too many good people.

Too many capable companies.

Playing the game alone.

They lose opportunities.

They lose time.

They lose partnerships.

A freight forwarding company in Australia, no matter how strong, can only fully serve Australia if it stands alone.

The moment shipments cross borders, **interdependence becomes unavoidable**.

That is where SGN comes in.

Through one shared ecosystem, a member instantly gains access to trusted partners across more than 90 countries—under one umbrella, one culture notice, one shared value system.

Not by owning everyone.

But by connecting everyone.

That is the power of interdependence.

From Coverage to Community

What surprised me most was not just the business growth.

It was what happened to people.

Companies that once operated in isolation now had:

- Wider reach
- Faster execution
- Stronger confidence

But more importantly, they gained **belonging**.

I've watched members travel overseas and call someone in the SGN family—not as a stranger, but as a friend.

I've seen fear replaced with familiarity.

Competition replaced with cooperation.

This is what happens when business becomes human again.

The journey is still early as along the way, as 90% people are still in a protective and self-defence mode. But once we meet anyone who think alike, the power is huge.

One of the biggest and oldest global networks in the world -- WCA, the owner and founder – David Yokeum who is 76 years old as I write this book, a legend himself, whom I had interviewed a few times, and I show high respect for.

He recently gifted me his signed book and I posted this to our LinkedIn Community:

Quote
So honoured to receive David's signed book today.
A true Logistics Legend — David Yokeum.

When I founded Signature Global Network (SGN), **<u>Signature Global Network PTY LTD</u>** *my focus was never "the business."*

It was always People. Culture. Connection.

So to those who are judging why I am speaking of other network owners: we are never in a competition with anyone else but ourselves! The world is so big if we build more things through interconnection and collaboration, not competition!!

My desire of starting my own network, the seed was planted 20 years ago at my very first WCAworld Conference.

I still remember walking into a room that felt like the United Nations of logistics — CEOs from every corner of the world, shaking hands, building relationships, lifting one another up. "This is brilliant!" I said to myself.

My heart was full. My energy was sky-high. And a quiet voice inside me said:

"One day… you will build something that unites people too and different!"

When we speak about global networks, everyone knows WCAworld.

Everyone knows David Yokeum.

This post isn't about promotion — it's about honouring a man who reshaped an entire industry.

People see the height of his achievements…

but few know the sacrifices, the pressure, the decades of decision-making, and the weight of building a global family of freight forwarders.

David is a man with:
✨ *A gold heart*
✨ *Vision backed by execution*
✨ *Leadership that serves people first*
✨ *Deep love for his wife and sons*
✨ *Humility that never changes — no matter how high he climbs*

I'm privileged to have interviewed him multiple times.

The more time you spend with him, the more you feel his humanity, depth, and generosity.

I'll be reading this book and sharing my reviews — but today, I just want to celebrate him.

If David Yokeum has ever inspired you, helped you, encouraged you, or shaped your logistics career…

Join me in the comments and write: RESPECT 🙏 so we can see what we can create together!

Let's honour those who built the path we're walking on today. I am sure you are one of them too!!
    unquote

This man is so successful that he does not need any more promotion, marketing or recognition, yet he still remains humble and open-minded to support the right course and the younger generations. The fact that he does not treat me as a competitor just as how I don't treat him as one shows our like-minded concept, which fills my soul.

We did not contact each other when I started the network and I was just doing what I was called to do. He spoke high of me and given me his signed book with special words, means a lot to me.

The reason I am sharing this with you is because I want you to know that there is a power when you treat NOBODY as your competitor. Your world is full of light, opportunities and open doors that nobody can stop you as you are no longer thinking for yourself but more for others and for the bigger purpose, for a better future of humanity. When you are silently building for a good course, the results will come, people are watching! Do not give up even if you haven't seen the ideal outcome yet!

The Bad Boss You Complained About & The Bad Staff You Complained About:

I have to address one of the biggest concerns I've witnessed in today's organizations.

    This is not just a workplace issue.

    It is a relationship issue.

    And it becomes toxic when the word *"toxic"* itself is misused.

    Let me share two stories.

Story 1 — For Employees

Shelly works for a global logistics company as a BDM. She has been with the company for about three years, and she complains about her boss constantly. She also complains about the company —about the culture, about the people. "It's so toxic!" she says.

One day, while chatting with colleagues behind her boss's back, she yelled:

"No boss is really good!"

"I hate my workplace. It's so toxic!"

"All my colleagues are toxic!"

Sarah, who was listening, paused. She had a completely different perspective.

Sarah gives thanks for her boss and the company she works for. She didn't argue with Shelly, because deep down she knew something important: like many others, Shelly does not enjoy working anywhere. No matter where she goes, she finds no purpose. Her *WHY* is fragile. She puts herself at the centre of the universe.

This mindset is often reinforced after attending certain seminars where overexcited coaches yell at audiences:

"You are the centre of the universe!"

Sarah believes that the moment she accepted the offer to join the company—even if the boss turned out to be a monster—she must take full ownership of her choice. Nobody pointed a gun at her and forced her to take the job.

In fact, she knows many people are not blessed or lucky enough to even have a job.

She can choose to leave or to stay—but whatever she chooses, she will be fully committed to it.

Every organization needs people like Sarah to flourish.

Nobody wants to hire people like Shelly.

The Moral of the Story

Many people today are living through hard seasons. Many work purely to earn money and nothing else. That is dangerous—because for most people, the time spent at work is far greater than the time spent with family.

When people face unfair treatment, setbacks, or life messes—and the pressure becomes too much—instead of changing their inner conversation or perspective, they choose to complain. Complaining reduces responsibility. They seek short-term external relief: entertainment, distraction, getting drunk, or blaming others.

What they forget is this:

Every relationship has **two parties**.

Each party carries **at least 50% responsibility** for any relationship they choose to stay in.

Life is always about choice.

In Christianity, God gives us free will—because without choice, we are no different from robots.

So here is the truth:

As an employee, **gratitude must be your number-one priority** when you choose to work for someone. Your greatest enemy—and joy-killer—is blaming others.

Happiness is often very simple.

It begins with inner gratitude.

The next time your mind fills with complaints—when you feel everyone is against you, taking advantage of you, or "toxic"— I'm sorry to say this, but maybe **you are part of the problem**.

Or maybe you are comparing yourself to others who seem to have better conditions, and you're focusing on what you lack.

Don't get me wrong—I am not saying you are not good or not enough. Your identity is shaped by what you believe about yourself and how you treat others.

I've been there.
I've played the victim.
I've hated my environment and the people in it.
The real problem is often not that your boss is toxic or the environment is toxic.
The real problem is **fear.**
Fear of saying no.
Fear of making a decision to leave or change.
Fear of facing the truth.
Do you know what *decide* really means?
To decide is to cut off other options.
When you choose A, you cut B, C, D, and E.
So my friend, out of love and respect:
If you find yourself calling others or your environment toxic, pause first. Appreciate what you have. Then be courageous enough to make real decisions and align with your *WHY.*
Your purpose will always guide you in the right direction.
I've experienced this myself. And every time I complained or judged others as if I were more perfect, I felt like slapping myself later. Because I was reminded of one thing:
I am responsible for every relationship within my control.
I must let go of what I cannot control.
And I must admit this truth:
The way I see others often reflects how others may see me.

In short:
Don't take anything for granted.
Everyone makes mistakes.
Treat others the way you want to be treated.
Be brave enough to make courageous decisions.
Live a purposeful life.

Story 2 — For Employers / Leaders
Paul was chatting with his friend Jack. Both are CEOs.

Paul: "Jack, I'm done with my staff member, Michael."
Jack: "Why?"

Paul: "No matter how much I give him, guide him, or mentor him, he doesn't change. He takes everything for granted."

Jack: "That's bad. Why don't you replace him?"

Paul: "Well… he still does some things better than others."

Jack: "Then it's your choice to keep using him."

Paul: "Man… he used to be good. Not anymore. He is toxic!"

Jack: "Did you ever try to understand why?"

Paul: "He used to be appreciative. Now he just wants more. He's greedy."

Jack (pauses): "This doesn't sound like a performance issue. It sounds like a human connection issue. When was the last calm one-on-one conversation you had with him?"

Paul: "It's been a while…"

Jack: "When was the last time you appreciated him publicly?"

Paul: "Um… Two years ago… I think." (looks sheepish)

Paul realized about things he hadn't done, so he went back and did his job as a leader.

He intentionally listened to Michael—and discovered that Michael was under enormous pressure. His mother was in hospital. His wife was pregnant. He was overwhelmed, losing passion, and battling mental health challenges.

After Paul's conversation and mentorship, Michael reconnected with his *WHY.*

Within three months, his performance increased fourfold.

Paul also intentionally moved Michael into a role that allowed more family time.

Paul realized something else too: he himself had been under extreme pressure to hit numbers. When Michael underperformed, Paul reacted with anger instead of understanding.

The good news?

Their relationship was restored.

The Moral of the Story

Leadership is about helping people find purpose.

Showing them a vision they cannot yet see.

Offering compassion.

Placing the right person in the right role at the right time.

It is never easy.

But it is always rewarding.

Interdependence cannot be removed from any organization or community.

As I often say to my team:

"We are one body. When the head is sick, the whole body suffers. When the hands stop moving, nothing gets done. When the legs don't listen to the brain, you cannot run."

The key is not to blame.

The key is not to escape.

The key is **win–win**, mutual support, and long-term thinking —**TOGETHER.**

Here are some core reasons why companies win together or fail alone:

1. Interdependence Inside Teams

I've seen this play out repeatedly inside SGN.

In one cross-country project, multiple companies from different regions worked together under shared responsibility.

No one asked, "Is this my job?"

They asked, "What does the team need right now?"

Because when people see themselves as part of something bigger than their title or company, something shifts.

Commitment deepens.

Ownership increases.

Results accelerate.

This is not theory.

It is lived experience.

The most successful teams don't rely on individual brilliance—they rely on **collective responsibility**.

2. Silos vs Unity

I've also seen the opposite.

Projects where teams worked in isolation.

Information was withheld.

Departments optimized their own outcomes instead of the company's future.

Everything slowed down.

Opportunities were missed.

Tension grew quietly.

It reminded me of something many great leaders have observed in different words over time:

When people protect their territory instead of the mission, progress stops.

Once knowledge, tools, and support systems were reintegrated—once people began sharing again—the same teams started winning.

Silos don't just slow companies down.

They quietly kill innovation.

Unity, on the other hand, multiplies what already exists.

3. Why Culture Beats Strategy Long-Term

I have seen companies with perfect strategies fail.

And companies with imperfect plans thrive.

The difference was never intelligence.

It was culture.

Culture is the invisible system holding all visible systems together.

You can copy strategies.

You can buy software.

You can hire talent.

But without trust, shared values, and mutual respect, nothing holds.

Some companies scale quickly—and then collapse just as fast—because culture was treated as an afterthought.

Others grow steadily, sustainably, and globally because people feel safe, seen, and responsible for one another.

As one legendary business leader once demonstrated through his teams:

Talent may win moments, but **teams that trust each other win eras**.

During my career time in a top global logistics company (global size up to 90,000 staff) when I worked as the Head of Trade reporting directly to the director of ANZ, I was invited to one culture meeting for all top management team members. There I shared my 6F culture framework, which I have shared with others and are used by global CEOs whom I ever taught. They are thriving by following these.

The 6 F words are:
Family (Belonging)
Faith (Trust)
Friendship(Bonding)
Fun (Energy & Passion)
Future (Growth & Development)
Fortune (Financial Development)

Following these 6F culture system, the company can thrive and create a health eco-system. It works for any company from a smaller size with about 5-10 staff up to 90,000+ staff.

When Competitors Become Ecosystems

One of the most powerful outcomes I've witnessed inside SGN is this:

Two companies meet as partners.
They collaborate.
They grow together.
Eventually, one opens a business in the other's country.

And instead of becoming enemies, they remain collaborators.

This is not weakness.

This is maturity.

Interdependence does not eliminate competition—it **evolves it**.

From "me versus you"

to

"us versus the problem."

That is how ecosystems are built.

Practical Framework: The Three Principles of Interdependent Companies

1. **Shared Responsibility**
   Everyone feels ownership—not just for their role, but for the outcome.
2. **Mutual Trust**
   Conflict is addressed, not avoided.
   People speak honestly, with respect.
3. **Celebrating Wins Together**
   Recognition reinforces unity.
   Shared success strengthens commitment.

These are not soft principles.
They are competitive advantages.

"Talent wins games, but teamwork wins championships." — *Michael Jordan*

I always say to my team that when we share joy, the joy multiplies, and when we share pain, the pain becomes less! Unity is always the biggest strength any household, school, company or organization could have.

When you read all those successful stories for the world biggest brands and most successful stories. Henry Ford hired the whole bunch of engineers and he was the one who believed and insisted, while the people who are doing the job and finding the way to make engine and four wheels are them.

If that does not prove that to succeed you must have a team, then how about Steve Jobs? He was the one who had all the ideas about computer, mobile phone and everything, but is he really the one who does the work? Steve Wozniak was the one who implemented, but why did people only remember Steve Jobs who already passed away while Steve Wozniak is still alive? Because a true leader is the one who dreams, who has visions, who believes and who has a whole bunch of team that will believe what he believes. The leader is the one who influences others to go one direction until they get there! Since you are reading this book, I assume that you are the leader, you are the changemaker and the chosen one! The key is – just because you are the chosen one doesn't mean you can get there unless you have a team with you!

I learned this a big time when I was still receiving spotlight for myself in my younger age. One day it just did not feel right for me to get those spotlights anymore. When my eyes are truly opened that I started seeing all amazingly successful people on the planet are giving thanks to their team and people behind them. Every. Single. One. No exceptional.

This touched me a lot. On 16th Nov 2025, Tom Cruise – the famous movie star received a lifetime achievement award given by the Academy of Motion Picture Arts and Sciences to those who have made "exceptional contributions to the state of motion picture arts and sciences." What surprised everyone but not surprised anyone is Tom's speech. During his 10 minutes speech, he said THANK YOU 20 times at least (roughly counting), and he almost thanked everyone there. He said nothing about himself but everyone else. This does not make him smaller or less, it indeed makes him bigger and more. I am not a professional actress or movie star, but looking at him doing these, I had to say to myself: "Wow, no doubt he won." He is not just winning. His inner circle is winning. They win together! No wonder they won!

When you walk alone, you cannot walk far enough; when you walk together, you walk forever. Success is only rewarding when you can share it with others, if success is simply your one-man show, there is no point to mention it at all.

No strategy can save a company whose people cannot stand together.
Interdependence turns competitors into ecosystems.
And ecosystems thrive where individuals alone eventually falter.
In business—just like in life—
we do not rise by standing apart, but by standing together.

WHY COMPANIES WIN TOGETHER OR FAIL ALONE

Interdependence turns competitors into ecosystems.

THE ILLUSION of WINNING ALONE

Heroic Founder   Dominant Company   Smartest in the Room

Fragmentation leads to **Weak Teams, Isolated Departments**

THE POWER of TOGETHER

Shared Ecosystem   Mutual Support   Collective Success

Unity leads to **Strong Culture, Lasting Growth**

FROM COMPETITORS TO ECOSYSTEMS

SILOS vs UNITY

SILOS & Division   Unity & Collaboration

THE 6F CULTURE

Family (Belonging)   Faith (Trust)   Friendship (Bonding)

Fun (Energy & Passion)   Future (Growth)   Fortune (Financial)

"TALENT WINS GAMES, BUT TEAMWORK WINS CHAMPIONSHIPS."

— Chapter 5 —

Why Companies Win Together or Fail Alone

Interdependence turns competitors into ecosystems.

My Notes/Take-aways

Chapter 6 — Love Your Enemy: A Living Lesson

Parable: The Bridge and the Fire
Two villages sat on opposite sides of a river.

For years, they traded, collaborated, and prospered together—until conflict arose.

Anger grew. Accusations flew. Eventually, one village burned the bridge between them, believing separation would bring safety.

At first, it felt powerful.

But soon, food became scarce. Trade stopped. Growth slowed.

When winter came, both villages suffered—not because of the river, but because the bridge was gone.

Interdependence doesn't disappear when bridges burn.

It simply turns into pain instead of progress.

From Companies to People
In Chapter 5, we explored a truth many leaders learn too late:

Companies don't fail because of strategy.

They fail because relationships break first.

Silos form. Trust erodes. Ego replaces humility.

And eventually, even the best systems collapse.

This chapter takes that same truth deeper—into **human behaviour.**

Because before silos exist in organisations, they exist in hearts.

Before companies fail alone, **people choose to disconnect first**.

To speak the fluent language of **Interdependence**, we must redefine love—not as softness, but as **courage**.

A Living Lesson at Our Front Door

One day, we were disturbed by someone pressing our doorbell almost five times.

Each time we opened the door, there was no one there.

Naturally, we started to get annoyed.

Finally, after the sixth time, Luke decided to hide and see who was doing it.

Three kids were caught.

They ran away so fast they even left their scooter behind.

Luke had to pretend to be angry so they would understand that what they did was inappropriate. We kept the scooter and waited, hoping one of them would come back to take responsibility.

Eventually, one little girl returned to say sorry.

Luke was amazed by her courage.

Of course, we forgave them.

Later that day, when Luke and I went out to buy Christmas gifts, we realized something remarkable—we were thinking of the **exact same Bible verse**, at the same time:

"But I tell you, love your enemies." — Matthew 5:44

When we acted on that verse, our kids were confused.

So I explained to them gently:

"Loving your enemy doesn't mean ignoring wrong behaviour.

It means responding with courage instead of retaliation."

Then they understood.

What began as an irritation became a **leadership lesson** — about accountability, forgiveness, and trust.

The same principles that build strong families…
Are the same principles that build enduring companies.

Why This Matters in Leadership and Business

I'm sharing this story because I truly believe we are all interconnected.

In business, we often speak about **partnerships, alliances, and ecosystems**.

But interdependence doesn't start in contracts — it starts in character.

Recently, witnessing deep tragedy close to home – the Bondi Beach Sydney shooting. It broke many hearts and shook many people's faith. That pain is real. But I don't believe losing faith — or losing humanity — is the answer.

When something painful happens in a household, we don't blame the house — we look at what the people inside need to heal.

Companies are no different.

When teams break down, when conflicts escalate, when cultures turn toxic — it's rarely a structural problem first.

It's a **relational one**.

Love Is a Leadership Discipline

History reminds us that loving your enemy is not weakness—it is **strategic courage**.

Nelson Mandela spent 27 years in prison, yet chose reconciliation over revenge. His leadership didn't just prevent civil war—it rebuilt an economy and a nation.

Abraham Lincoln filled his cabinet with former rivals. When questioned, he replied that he didn't want to destroy his enemies—he wanted to turn them into allies.

Great leaders understand this truth:

What you refuse to heal, you will eventually repeat — at scale.

In companies, unresolved resentment becomes silos.

In teams, unhealed ego becomes turnover.
In leaders, unforgiveness becomes isolation.

Choosing a Different First Response

What if more leaders chose courage over control?

What if empathy, awareness, and responsibility became our **first response**, instead of fear and blame?

I'm not perfect. I'm also guilty—working too much, being distracted, not always being fully present. None of us are exceptions. We are human.

But maybe—just maybe—if we all contributed a little more…

Maybe—just maybe – if some of us are neighbours of those shooters and gave them some extra love before that tragedy happened?

Maybe—just maybe– if some more heroes that day instead of escaping, ran to those shooters and worked strategically together, will that save at least a few more lives?

The Ants Metaphor — Small Alone, Unstoppable Together

There is something I often reflect on when I think about interdependence.

Ants.

A single ant is fragile.

It can be crushed easily.

It cannot carry much.

It cannot survive long on its own.

But when ants come together—something extraordinary happens.

They carry objects many times heavier than their own bodies.

They build complex structures without a leader shouting orders.

When danger appears, they don't panic or scatter—they **organize**.

They form bridges with their own bodies.
They protect the weakest.
They move as one.
Ants don't ask, *"What's in it for me?"*
They act because the **colony matters**.

Now pause—and think about us.

What if more of us chose courage over control?

What if empathy, awareness, and responsibility became our first response instead of fear and blame?

Maybe—just maybe—if some of us had noticed the loneliness, the anger, the isolation in others earlier…

Maybe—just maybe—if more love, connection, and care had reached them before pain exploded…

Maybe—just maybe—if more people had stood together instead of running alone, more lives could have been protected.

This is not about heroism.

This is about **collective responsibility**.

If ants—creatures so small—can work together instinctively for survival,

what excuse do we, as humans, have?

Unexpected Outcome

Two days after we gave the gifts, those same kids came back again—knocking on our door repeatedly.

This time, they weren't playing tricks.

They invited my kids to be friends.

They even brought gifts for my children.

We never expected that.

I was speechless.

This is how interdependence works in real life—and in business.

When trust is extended first, cooperation often follows.

When forgiveness leads, collaboration multiplies.

Love doesn't weaken systems.

It restores them.

Interdependence Is Not Optional

Interconnection matters because we truly need each other.

Different cultures, backgrounds, opinions, and stories are not barriers—they are assets.

Every person you meet carries something unseen.

Every organisation carries unresolved stories beneath the surface.

That's why leadership is not power over people.

It is **responsibility for people**.

A Call to United Leadership

My friend—you are courageous.

I am courageous.

And together, we are stronger.

We either build the future together—with faith and courage—or we fragment it with fear and blame.

Wherever there are people, there are problems.

But there is also love, purpose, and fulfilment.

It's time to stand more united—for our businesses, our families, and the next generation.

Let us not blame, but support one another.

Let us not chase only personal wins, but long-term shared success.

Let us not push others down, but lift each other up.

Because if I don't do it, others may not.

If you don't do it, others may not.

Leadership always starts somewhere.

It starts with **you and me**.

We are all drops of water.

And together—we form the ocean.

If we chose to be **givers**, not just achievers…

More people would feel safe, valued, and committed.

That's when performance rises naturally.

Let love rule over hate.

Let faith rule over fear.

Let us become living examples.

— Chapter 6 —

Love Your Enemy: A Living Lesson

*Parable: **The Bridge and the Fire***

— **Thriving** together across a bridge of trust. —

One **village burned the bridge,**
believing separation brought **safety.**

Trade stopped. **Food grew scarce.**
Both suffered in **isolation.**

— A Living Lesson —

"Destroying bridges is easy, but **rebuilding them requires courage.**"

— **Why This Matters in Leadership** —

Interdependence doesn't end when **bridges burn**—it just turn into **pain instead** of progress.
Great leaders don't win by **destroying enemies.** They win by **confronting ego,**
anger, and fear—starting with their **own.**

— **What Ants Teach Us** —

- Small Alone, Unstoppable Together
- Carry what **they cannot alone.**
- Build **bridges** with their bodies.
- Protect the **colony** without **ego.**

A single ant is fragile. But together, they thrive—demonstrating
the power of unity.

My Notes/Take-aways

Chapter 7 — We Are All Carrying Something

Everyone Leaks Pain

Can you stop thinking that nobody understands about your pain or you are the only one who suffers pain? Pain is not short for supply. Every person you meet is carrying something unseen.

Some carry trauma from childhood.
Some carry heartbreak from lost opportunities or relationships.
Some carry fear wrapped in anger.

Even the most successful leaders, the most confident CEOs, the people you think "have it all"—they leak pain in ways you might never notice. I've been working with multinational global CEOs. I've always been close to the owners and CEOs and hearing their hidden pains and struggles. It is not a sign of weakness, it is simply a sign of humanity. If you never feel pain, you are either not a human, or you are sick.

I've learned the lessons of pain the hard way myself. My own past shaped my reactions long before I was aware of it. There were moments I responded with frustration, impatience, or anger—and later realized it was **fear masquerading as force**.

The truth is simple but humbling: **we are all fragile. We are all human. And we all need one another.**

If we already know pain exists, why are we frustrated when

it comes? We shouldn't be surprised, and as if it never happened before. As I mature, I managed my response to pain more calmly.

But here is the trick many people are still living in it.
    The more we say:
    "I don't need you!"
    "Leave me alone!"
    or anything like that, it is simply directing to one truth and the truth is the opposite –
    "I need you."
    "Be with me and accompany me."
    I don't know why this happens to humans, and it is still a human mystery.

Every time when I was mad at my husband, I would say these opposite words and knowing that I was just mad at him, but him – the wise man, after suffering many times before, learned a big time, will stay more when I say those words. We do not fight much at all, it is just some days when I was not in the mood, and when I feel distanced, I would say words to protect my egos. We both know these are all words that need the opposite understandings.

Are you familiar? If you have these moments too, remember if you love someone, when they say those words, it does not mean that they are mean to you, they are rude, or they do not care about you. The fact is they care about you so much that their ego does not want to face the truth. If you ever learn from this, remember – to be kind to those who love you and you love.

Personal Reflection — My Journey of Awareness

Early in my life, I carried loneliness like a secret backpack. It weighed me down in ways I didn't even notice.

I took being independent as my badge of pride. Whenever I talked to someone, I'd emphasis how early I took care of myself since an age of 17 and even took care of my parents… these are all true, but the way how I say it does not make myself look that good after all. I was still carrying some weight from the past… some pain that I thought I had let go but hadn't yet. Don't feel bad, my friend, because healing is a process, particularly the childhood pain and trauma, sometimes it takes a lifetime. We are not here to heal the past, we are here to be aware so that we can intentionally give opportunity of our present and future to have more of our attention. ***The past is gone, the present is now and the future is coming.***

In leadership, I saw others carrying burdens too. Teams had unspoken fears, unacknowledged frustrations, or unresolved conflicts.

I once observed a team in Australia — brilliant individuals, top performers — but when silos formed, productivity dropped and morale plummeted. It wasn't because the people were incapable. It was because **unspoken struggles leaked into every interaction.**

It reminded me of something I read about the Dalai Lama: *"Be kind whenever possible. It is always possible."*

Kindness is not naive. It is **the first step to healing the invisible wounds around us.**

Community Insight — Healing People, Not Just Structures

I do not read news because I believe it will only weigh us down and create more fear, but when things happen around you, you can hardly ignore them. What I do believe is to learn from every lesson in history, not to dwell on the past complaining and be controlled by fear from the media. Looking at it as a historical story to learn and reflect and see how we can do better.

On 27th Nov 2025, according to ABC/BBC and all global news, at least 83 people passed away and about 200+ are missing, following a fire in Hong Kong.

Three men involved with a construction company suspected of negligence have been arrested. The fire at the Wang Fuk Court complex might have been caused by a "grossly negligent" construction firm using unsafe materials, the police alleged.

This news is true as we also have relatives in Hong Kong. Thank God that they are OK.

When something goes wrong in a home, we don't blame the house—we look at the people inside.

If people are aware of the potential risk of using the cheap materials, the disaster wouldn't happen. Imagining 83 people and 200+ are still unaccountable as well as the families who are related to these 283+ people.

The same applies to companies, communities or countries.

The crazy thing is that most of us complain about our country and government while forgetting that is the thing we have. Or students or teachers complain about schools or staff complains about the company. It is brutally true but sad that sometimes we all make mistakes. Sometimes it is the foolishness, greed or personal interest that directed people to make mistakes and wrong decisions. The question is not what others can do for us and what government, companies, schools can do for us. The question is really what can we do to achieve better goals TOGETHER?

It is just like we live in a household, and when something goes wrong, we complain about our house. The fact is the family members in the household. The crucial question is how much we involved and how interdependent are we?

We don't fix walls; we **heal hearts**.

We don't just repair systems; we **restore trust**.

I've seen communities rebuild after tragedies, and companies turn around, not because new rules were imposed, but because leaders and teams **noticed the human pain first** and **responded with empathy**.

Even small actions—listening without judgment, offering help without expectation, forgiving before being asked—have ripple effects that can change lives and transform organizations.

Consider **Fred Rogers**, known as Mr. Rogers. His entire career revolved around understanding the invisible struggles of children. He taught that everyone is carrying something, and even the smallest acts of kindness and acknowledgment can make a world of difference.

Or look at **Howard Schultz**, former CEO of Starbucks. He focused on building a company culture where employees felt seen, heard, and valued — he understood that a happy, cared-for workforce would create an ecosystem of care for customers.

Both understood that **systems succeed when people are healed and supported first.**

Kindness Must Come Before Judgment

We often rush to judge what we don't understand.

We criticize, we compare, we label.

But judgment without awareness only deepens isolation.

Kindness comes first.

Awareness comes first.

Compassion comes first.

Because if we can see that everyone is carrying something—sometimes invisible, sometimes heavy—we learn to respond differently.

We begin to **listen before correcting, support before criticizing, and forgive before punishing.**

That is the invisible language of interdependence.

That is the work that transforms families, teams, and communities.

"You are so judgemental!" My daughter said that to me a few times, and so is a few of my friends. It is a human nature, but I learned to change, because what I have learned is that just like what the bible says "Don't judge or you will be judged." It is so true that it seems if ever I judged someone for anything, it will come back to me one day.

I often say to myself the reminder of "Life is just like a mirror, when you smile, it smiles back at you; when you frown, it frowns back." From that moment, I am constantly carrying the reminder of compassion. Being kind to anyone as much as possible, because we don't know what is happening in their life and behind the scenes.

Kindness must come before judgment. This principle serves me with wise decisions and behaviours. It helps me to avoid jumping to conclusion too quickly, but allowing time of understanding about humanity and creating wisdom to play with win-win outcomes.

— Chapter 7 —
Everyone Is Carrying Something —
Pain Is Invisible, But Humanity Is Shared

The Hidden Reality
Even the strongest leaders leak pain
• trauma, fear
• loss
• loneliness

Awareness Before Healing
Healing Begins with Awareness
• respond instead of react
• soften instead of defend
• connect instead isolate

We Are All Carrying Something
• Past trauma
• Hidden fear
• Silent struggle

Kindness Before Judgment
We Notice Hearts Before Systems
• Listen before judging
• Understand before correcting

Pain is often unseen
• Past trauma
• Hidden fear
• Silent struggle

Kindness Before Judgment
• We Istean before puinishing
• Understand before correcting
• Support before blaming

When We Lead with Awareness, Pain Becomes Connection.
Pain is not a personal failure—it is a human experience.
When we respond with kindness, we unlock the true power of
Interdependence.

— Interdependence by Kristy Guo —

— Chapter 7 —
Everyone Is Carrying Something —
Pain Is Invisible, But Humanity Is Shared

Trauma
Loss
Fear
Loneliness

1 The Hidden Burden
Pain is invisible but universal. Everyone you meet is carrying a hidden burden.
Fear
Trauma
Loss
Trauma, Loss, Fear, Loneliness

2 Beneath the Mask
Even strong leaders leak their pain in quiet ways.
"Leave me alone."
"I don't need you."

3 The Core Paradox
People often say the opposite of what they need.
Please stay.
Please understand me"

4 What People Really Need
It's not judgment they seek—it's awareness, kindness, and listening.
• Listening instead of judging
• Understanding instead of criticizing
• Supporting instead of blaming

Pain is not a personal failure—it is a human experience.
When we lead with awareness, pain becomes connection.

We don't heal systems. We heal people. And people heal systems.

Interdependence
BY KRISTY GUO

My Notes/Take-aways

Chapter 8 — Faith Over Fear

When Pain Shakes Faith, Systems Fracture

There is a Chinese Proverb once said: **"It is always easy to fall in love but harder to live together."** It is very true, because wherever two different individuals come together, it will potentially have miss-understandings, different opinions, and different perspectives and all of these will cause PAIN.

Pain does not just shake individuals.
It shakes systems.
It shakes families.
It shakes teams.
It shakes nations.

When pain enters a system and faith disappears, something dangerous happens -- **people turn inward.**

They protect themselves.
They isolate.
They stop trusting.
That is why pain doesn't just create suffering — it creates **fragmentation**.

I've watched people say, *"I lost my faith after tragedy."*
What they often mean is: *"I stopped believing we are held together."*

But here is the truth I've learned through life and leadership:
Pain may shake faith — but abandoning faith breaks interdependence.
And when interdependence breaks, fear takes over.

In my life, I've seen people giving up dreaming big because of fearing to lose what they already have; I've seen people live life one day at a time because they lose faith of the future which is the hope. I've seen people playing small because they fear of lacking if there is any risk so they'd rather not change. We all had these moments in certain areas of life when we make choices, simply because we are humans. But if we are not careful and if we let fear take over in relationships, trust breaks, marriage, friendship, partnerships are all fragile.

I've seen people abandon faith because of what's happening around them, and the most I've heard was: "If God is real, why does he allow bad things happen?" It is always easier to blame someone especially God when something does not go along your way. I do not have all the answers but what I do know is that looking back at my own journey, growth never comes after painless comfort zone, it always comes after pains. No pain, no gain. It sounds easy for me to say it, I know, but I suffered doubts and fear too, and what I have learned is that when you believe, you achieve! If I believe in something positive will happen, it will, and if I believe in something negative will happen, it will.

Faith to me is the most beautiful gift we can have. It is unshakable and it is the best shield for me to defend my hope for the future even when I am facing a temporary setback, instead of being defeated, I am only detoured, and I will always get there!

"Faith is taking the first step even when you don't see the whole staircase."— **Martin Luther King Jr.**
Faith may not be able to answer all your doubts or questions, but it knows where to go, despite the storms or set-backs.

Faith is powerful because it is not seen but you still need to believe. Successful people walk by faith, not by sight. The reward of faith is to believe in advance what you haven't seen in your eyes but seen in your mind!

I believe faithful people let future lead, but fearful people let past lead. Most of the time the reason why people are fearful is because of the past experience. Faith is not the opposite to fear, it is simply the existence of trusting despite the existence of fear. Life is full of storms, uncertainties and dramas, but faith reminds us of who is really in control. Once our faith is strong enough, we shall find the deepest and firmest inner peace that is unshakable despite any circumstance.

Personal Faith Journey — When I Could Not Carry Life Alone

There were seasons in my life when independence was impossible.

Leaving home.

Starting again in Australia, in a new city, with zero friends, and no family support.

Facing exams before I could make it to Australia;

Failed my driving license test 6-7 times altogether (writing and road tests.)

Got a massive car accident.

Had to deal with language and culture barriers (Despite my English was pretty okay before I immigrated, it took a while to understand Aussie English and the culture.)

Financial pressure – working for a company that only paid me a basic salary but we had to pay house rent, childcare payment, etc.)

Fear of losing my job – The loneliness I had to deal with when seeing everyone got off around 4:45pm, I sat on my desk, finished all my work an hour ago, but didn't dare to leave until 5pm.

A voice is telling me: "What if they don't think you are valuable enough? What if they send you back and you will never get your citizenship here?"

Logic told me: *"You are on your own."*

Fear whispered: *"You must survive alone."*

But faith showed me something else:

I was never carrying life by myself.

People showed up – when I opened up my mind and eyes, I realized that I am living in a beautiful country, Australia, where I've never seen such a group of generous people before.

The multinationalism, the diversity, the culture of support and love.

Opportunities appeared unexpectedly. I would never be able to get these opportunities when I was in China or Hong Kong.

Strength came from places I didn't manufacture. The more I do, the more confident I become. The more I try, the more faithful I become.

Faith, for me, was not about certainty.

It was the quiet belief that **I was part of something larger than myself** — that even when I couldn't see the system, I was still inside it.

That belief kept me moving forward when isolation would have crushed me.

I remember there's one day after living in Australia for 1 year and we were still waiting for our PR to come, with so much pressure from everywhere. I felt overwhelmed, and when looking around the city of Melbourne and the people, I suddenly felt disconnected and I started to doubt myself – *Am I really coming to the right place? I used to being at the top of the world, I got high pay, high position, and a whole bunch of old connections of friends and families around…* I started to believe that I was alone and I have to survive alone. Of course my victim mindset came to play… I burst into tears but when seeing my little kid and my loving husband, I just got up and kept going.

But I remember the day when I was invited to the business trip and the day when the team celebrated me for my 1 year anniversary, I started to open up myself. Later even when my parents came to visit, they even asked me to take them to the office and visited me. I realized that it is not they who excludes me, but me who excludes myself. I dwelled on my past habits, culture and ways. The moment when I embrace the 'new' and let go the 'old,' and treated where I am and people around me as my family, everything changed.

So every time when fear comes to play and speaking to me, the conversation will be like this: *Well, I am already interconnected with all of them; They all know me; It is not just a loss for me if I am not staying here, it will also be their huge loss!* That faith carries me all the way and my ID was applied within two years and we got the PR within only three years and later citizenship.

Do you know? Faith and fear are both beliefs. The difference is one is believing in a positive outcome that will do your favour, and the other one is believing in a negative outcome that will be against your ideal outcome. The moment when I switched my mindset, replaced my focus on the negative outcome with the positive outcome, everything changed. That faith covers me every day and directs me with the best attitude and the decisions I make daily.

If I'd allow fear to carry me, I would not be here writing this book as I wouldn't have even come to Australia or stayed in Australia and my whole story would be rewritten. My questions for you is: **will you allow fear or faith to carry your future?**

The Bridge We Cross Together

Faith is often described as a bridge in the fog.

But here is what we forget:

No bridge is built for one person.
Bridges exist because communities need connection.
Faith works the same way.
When visibility disappears, fear says: *"Save yourself."*
Faith says: *"Move together."*
Every step forward was possible because others had crossed before me — and because someone would cross after me.
That is interdependence.

Sacrifice as the Highest Form of Interdependence

At the heart of nearly every belief system is the same message:

One carries pain so many can live.

In Christianity, God's sacrifice is not just spiritual — it is the ultimate picture of interdependence:
One life offered so relationship could be restored.
One sacrifice so separation could end.

This pattern repeats everywhere:

- Parents sacrificing comfort for children
- Leaders absorbing pressure so teams can survive
- Individuals choosing forgiveness so communities don't collapse

Faith is not about personal salvation alone.
Faith is about **choosing responsibility for the whole**.
That is interdependence at its highest level.

When Faith Collapses, So Does Unity

History teaches us something uncomfortable but clear:
Civilizations do not fall when they lose power.
They fall when they lose **shared meaning**.
When people stop believing they belong to one another, fear replaces trust.

Fear creates enemies.

Enemies justify destruction.

Viktor Frankl observed that people survived unimaginable suffering not because they were stronger — but because they believed their lives were connected to something beyond themselves.

Nelson Mandela chose reconciliation because he understood this truth:

Without shared faith in humanity, freedom would destroy itself.

Faith is the *operating system* that allows interdependence to function at scale.

Faith vs Fear — A Leadership and Systems Lens

Fear-based leadership fractures systems.

Faith-based leadership holds them together.

Fear asks:

- *Who can I trust?*
- *Who might betray me?*
- *How do I protect myself?*

Faith asks:

- *Who am I responsible for?*
- *How do we move forward together?*
- *What must I carry so others can stand?*

This is why fear creates silos in companies.

Why resentment creates turnover.

Why isolation always follows unforgiveness.

What leaders refuse to heal, organizations repeat — at scale.

Faith is not soft.

Faith is **systemic courage**.

Choosing Interdependence

Faith is not pretending everything will be okay.

Faith is choosing to stay connected when fear tells you to withdraw.

It is choosing:

- Meaning over isolation
- Responsibility over blame
- Humanity over self-protection

Because fear fractures systems.
But faith holds people together.

"Faith is choosing shared meaning — and choosing one another — even when logic fails."

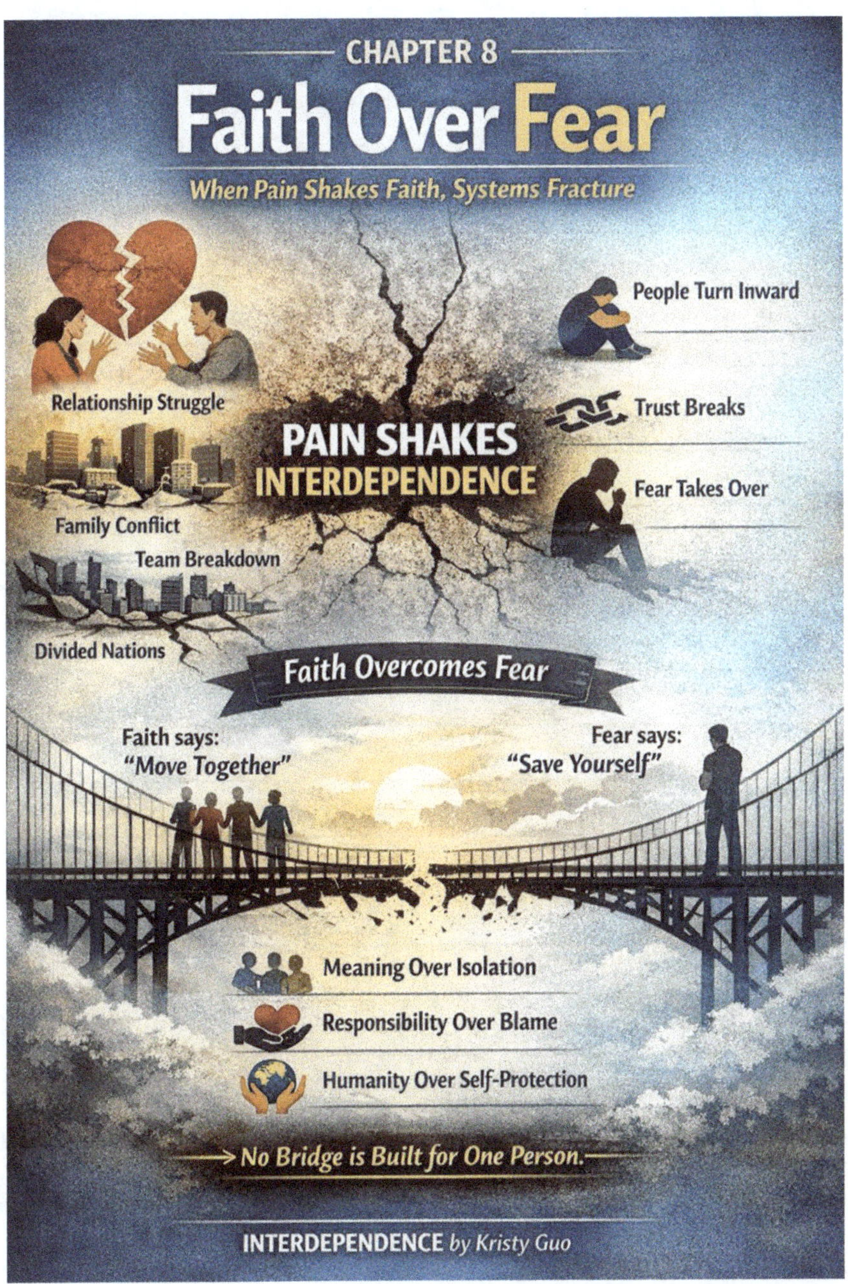

CHAPTER 8
Faith Over Fear
When Pain Shakes Faith, Systems Fracture
Relationship Struggle
Family Conflict
Team Breakdown
Divided Nations
PAIN SHAKES INTERDEPENDENCE
People Turn Inward
Trust Breaks
Fear Takes Over
Faith Overcomes Fear
Faith says: "Move Together"
Fear says: "Save Yourself"
Meaning Over Isolation
Responsibility Over Blame
Humanity Over Self-Protection
No Bridge is Built for One Person.
INTERDEPENDENCE by Kristy Guo

My Notes/Take-aways

Chapter 9 — Purpose Is a Shared Responsibility Life Is Short, Legacy Is Long

If I ask you to use ChatGPT and ask this question, will that change a bit of your thinking about life?

This is what I typed:
"I am turning 40 in 8 months, and I need to know if as an average age of human being's lifespan, how many years, months, days, and hours I have left on earth? Show me by using also chart, diagram and graph."

These are what I got from CHATGPT (Let us not believe 100% about what CHATGPT says but it is a great reference)

CHATGPT says:
QUOTE

Here's a **personalized life-expectancy estimate** based on the *average human lifespan* — and then visualized with simple charts and graphs. This is *statistical* and *not a prediction of your actual life* (many factors like health, genetics, lifestyle, country, etc. influence real lifespan).

🎯 1. Assumptions

- **Your current age:** ~39 years (turning 40 in 8 months)

- **Average global life expectancy: ~73 years**
  (World Health Organization estimate; varies by country)
- **Remaining life (statistical average):**
  ~73 − 40 = **33 years**

📌 **2. Time Remaining (Estimated)**

Unit	Amount
Years	33
Months	33 × 12 = **396 months**
Days	33 × 365.2425 ≈ **12,042 days**
Hours	12,042 × 24 ≈ **289,008 hours**

Note: We used an average year length including leap years: **365.2425 days**

📊 **3. Simple Timeline Chart**

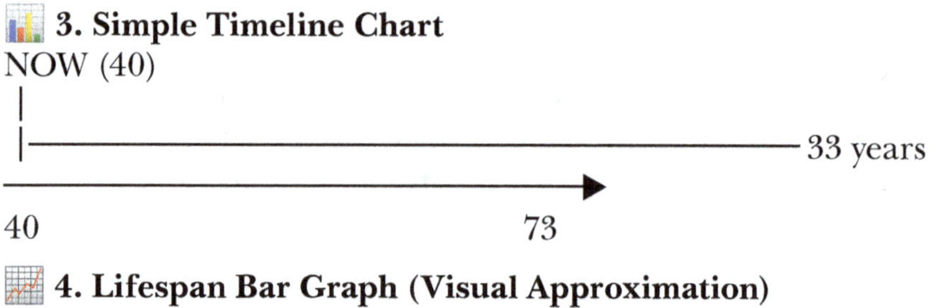

📈 **4. Lifespan Bar Graph (Visual Approximation)**
Age 0
|■■■■■■■■■■■■■■■■■■■■■■■■■■■■■■| 100
　　0　　　40　　　73

Legend:
■■■■ = Years lived
---- = Years remaining (estimated)
In this chart:

- The **first 40 years** are the past
- The **next 33 years** are your statistical expected future
- After 73 would be beyond the *global average*

You can think of it like a progress bar:

Past (0–40)   Lived: ███████████████████████████ (40)
Future (40–73) Left: ███████████████████████ (33)
Beyond Average   —

5. Proportional Pie (Text-Style)

[████████████████████████████████] 55% Lived
[███████████████████████] 45% Expected Remaining

- **~55%** of average lifespan completed
- **~45%** remaining (statistical estimate)

UNQUOTE

Life is fragile, life is short.
One phone call can change everything.
One moment can divide "before" and "after."
We don't get to choose how long we live — but we do choose **what continues after us**.

Legacy is not built by how much we accumulate.
It is built by **who is lifted because we were here**.
This is where interdependence becomes unavoidable:
No legacy is created alone.
No purpose survives isolation.
Purpose only outlives us when it is **shared, carried, and multiplied by others**.

The Great Lie About Purpose

Modern culture teaches us to *find* our purpose — as if it is hidden somewhere inside us, waiting to be discovered.
But here is the truth I've lived:
Purpose is not found in isolation.
Purpose is revealed through responsibility to others.

Your purpose shows up when:

- Someone needs your voice
- Someone needs your courage
- Someone needs what you've already survived

Purpose is not about self-expression.
It is about **service within a system**.
That is interdependence.

My Mission — Turning Success Into Shared Legacy

As my world expanded — businesses, stages, networks, countries — one question became impossible to ignore:

What happens if I succeed, but others are left behind?

That question reshaped everything.

My mission became clear:

- Elevate others, not compete with them
- Share platforms, not protect them
- Turn untold stories into legacies

This is why *Signature Global Network* was never built as a company alone — but as a **community**.

This is why *The Logistics Legend Series* exists — not to spotlight me, but to preserve the impact of others.

Because success that dies with one person is not success.

It is an **unfinished responsibility**.

I've never shared this with anyone until now:

When I first published my books, I felt super fulfilled, I felt proud, and all spotlights went to me -- that felt amazing! Not until I started the co-author program when I gathered around 7 co-authors to write books together with me and when I saw their life transformed significantly. I no longer wanted to be spotlighted. I intentionally avoided any praise to myself... I just didn't feel happy for any recognition. Instead, when seeing those who participated to the program getting more opportunities, opening doors and recognition, my heart is full. That is why we published The Logistics Legends, then the Logistics Legends Volume 2 and also The World's Thought Leaders. Man, these amazing people have so many stories! Every story touched me so much! They are so powerful!

Honestly, if I never did this co-author journey with them, I would probably still dwell in the little spotlight of becoming an author and writing books to help people, but I would never discover the deeper side of it – the interconnection and interdependence of purpose and sense of achievement. The sense of joy that fulfills me would never happen if it is just about myself.

A Quiet Truth — Saving Lives Rarely Looks Dramatic

We often imagine purpose as something heroic.
Saving lives.
Changing history.
Standing on stages.

But most of the time, purpose looks much quieter.
It looks like:

- Listening when someone feels invisible
- Opening a door for someone with no access
- Believing in someone before they believe in themselves

Some of the most powerful moments I've witnessed didn't involve applause.
They involved presence.
And presence is the currency of interdependence.
Ask yourself: "When was I felt fulfilled like a hero last time? What did I do?" It doesn't have to be huge… maybe a kind message of encouragement to your staff? Maybe say to someone that you believe in them?

A Parable — The Torch That Couldn't Burn Alone

There is an old parable about a single torch trying to light a valley.
No matter how strong the flame, the darkness remains vast.

But when torches are passed — from one person to another — the valley begins to glow.

Purpose works the same way.
One life can spark meaning.
Many lives carry it forward.

If you hold the flame but refuse to pass it, the light ends with you.
If you share it, the light becomes a system.

Interdependence and Legacy — Why Purpose Must Be Shared

Legacy is not what people remember about you.
Legacy is what **continues without you**.
That only happens when:

- Knowledge is shared
- Power is distributed
- Responsibility is multiplied

This is why:

- Parents shape generations
- Leaders shape cultures
- Communities shape civilizations

Purpose is never a solo assignment.
It is a **relay**.
And interdependence is the mechanism that allows it to travel.

Leadership Reflection — What You Lift, Lifts You

In leadership, purpose is often mistaken for vision.
But vision without responsibility creates followers.
Responsibility creates **builders**.
True leaders don't ask:

- *How far can I go?*

They ask:

- *How many can rise with me?*

Because whatever you lift will eventually lift you.

And whatever you ignore will one day weaken the system you stand on.

The Responsibility Is Ours

We don't choose whether our lives affect others.

They already do.

The only choice we have is **how**.

Will we:

- Compete or contribute?
- Accumulate or multiply?
- Protect or pass on?

Purpose does not belong to you alone.

It belongs to everyone your life touches.

"Purpose multiplies when shared — and legacy is born when we carry it together."

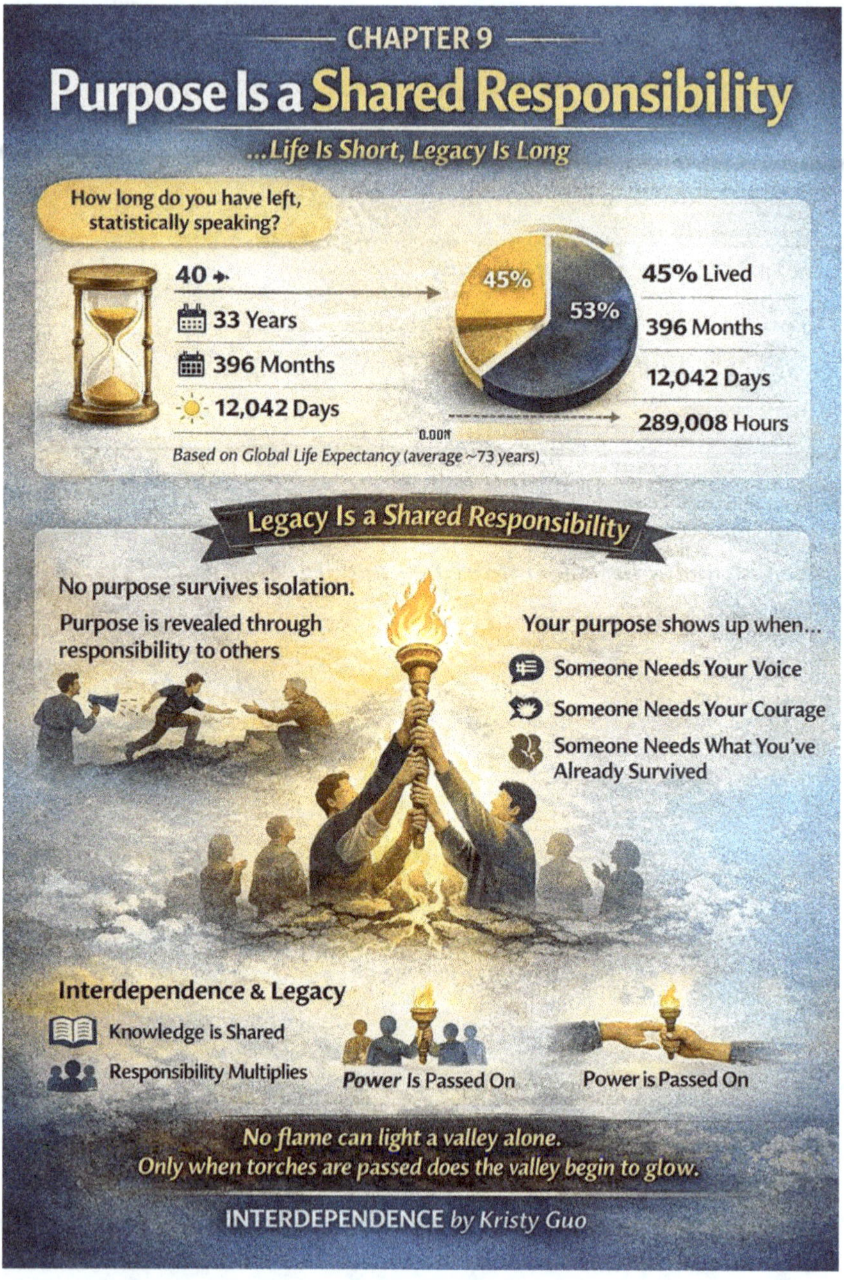

CHAPTER 9

Purpose Is a Shared Responsibility

...Life Is Short, Legacy Is Long

How long do you have left, statistically speaking?

40 ➜

- 📅 33 Years
- 📅 396 Months
- ☀️ 12,042 Days

45%

53%

0.00%

- **45%** Lived
- **396** Months
- **12,042** Days
- **289,008** Hours

Based on Global Life Expectancy (average ~73 years)

Legacy Is a Shared Responsibility

No purpose survives isolation.

Purpose is revealed through responsibility to others

Your purpose shows up when...

- Someone Needs Your Voice
- Someone Needs Your Courage
- Someone Needs What You've Already Survived

Interdependence & Legacy

- Knowledge is Shared
- Responsibility Multiplies

Power Is Passed On

Power is Passed On

No flame can light a valley alone.
Only when torches are passed does the valley begin to glow.

INTERDEPENDENCE *by Kristy Guo*

My Notes/Take-aways

From Philosophy to Practice

Interdependence is not something you agree with.
It is something you practice — daily, intentionally, imperfectly.

Chapter 10 — The Global Language of Interdependence

Purpose of This Chapter

To show that **interdependence is universal** — transcending culture, religion, politics, or ideology — and that most human tragedies are not caused by a lack of intelligence, but by a **failure of connection**.

We do not suffer because we are stupid.

We suffer because we forget we belong to one another.

Key Questions This Chapter Answers

- Why people across cultures ultimately want the same things
- Why division always comes *before* collapse
- Why interdependence is humanity's oldest — and most reliable — survival system

Section 1 — One World, One Human Language

I've worked with leaders across 90+ countries.

Different passports.

Different religions.

Different accents.

Different histories.
Yet the *same questions* repeat everywhere:

- Am I enough?
- Do I belong?
- Who will stand with me when I fail?

Strip away titles, uniforms, borders, and LinkedIn profiles — and underneath, we all want the same things.

Universal Human Needs

Across every culture, humans seek:

- Safety
- Belonging
- Dignity
- Purpose
- Contribution

When these needs are met, people cooperate.
When they are denied, something else rises.

When These Needs Are Denied

- Fear increases
- Identity hardens
- Blame becomes easier than understanding
- Conflict begins

Wars do not start with weapons.
They start when people stop seeing each other as **human**.
Once someone becomes a label — enemy, outsider, problem — empathy switches off.
And history tells us exactly where that leads.

Section 2 — Why Interdependence Transcends Culture, Race, and Religion

From Asia to Europe,

From Africa to the Americas,
From boardrooms to villages:

- Parents want their children safe
- Leaders want respect, not rebellion
- Communities want stability
- People want to be seen

Different languages.
Same emotional operating system.

A Practical Reframe

Let's simplify something we often overcomplicate:

- **Independence** says: *"I don't need you."*
- **Dependence** says: *"I cannot survive without you."*
- **Interdependence** says:
  "We are stronger because we choose one another."

This is not weakness.
This is **design**.
Jim Rohn said it best in one of his seminar recordings:
"Instead of saying: I will take care of myself and you will take care of yourself, let's say:
'Hey, how about I will take care of myself FOR YOU, so that you can take care of yourself FOR ME?'"
This is genius.
Not because it sounds nice —but because **it works**.
Interdependence aligns self-interest with collective good.
No ideology does this better.

Section 3 — Why Interdependence Prevents Wars and Tragedies

Every large-scale tragedy in human history shares the same root:

- Dehumanization
- Isolation
- "Us vs Them" thinking

When interdependence is forgotten:

- Leaders sacrifice people to protect power
- Systems protect profit over dignity
- Fear becomes policy
- Silence becomes compliance

And the most dangerous phrase appears:
"This doesn't concern me."

What Interdependence Restores

- Listening before reacting
- Mutual responsibility
- Shared consequences

You do not destroy what you feel responsible for.
You protect it.
You invest in it.
You pause before harming it.
Interdependence doesn't remove conflict — it removes **indifference**.
And indifference is what kills societies quietly.

Section 4 — The Interdependence Scale (Global Version)

Workbook Tool: Global Interdependence Audit
Rate yourself honestly from **1 (rarely)** to **5 (always)**:

- I seek to understand before judging
- I recognise how my success impacts others
- I speak up when exclusion is happening
- I build bridges instead of camps
- I treat strangers as future allies

Score Interpretation

- **20–25**: Actively strengthening humanity

- **10–19**: Neutral — but neutrality still has consequences
- **Below 10**: Isolation quietly shapes your worldview

This is not a moral scorecard.
It's a **mirror**.

Section 5 — One Small Action That Changes the System

You don't need a global position to create global impact.
Choose **one**:

- Listen to someone you deeply disagree with — **without trying to win**
- Support a cause that does not benefit you directly
- Teach your child compassion through action, not lectures
- Replace criticism with curiosity — especially at work

Global change is the accumulation of personal choices.
Interdependence is not a theory.
It is humanity's **operating language**.

Practical Guiding Questions (For Reflection or Team Discussion)

Use these questions personally — or bring them into leadership meetings, team workshops, or boardrooms:

1. Where in my life or organisation have we prioritised efficiency over dignity?
2. Who benefits from our success — and who is invisible in the process?
3. Where has "us vs them" quietly appeared in our culture?
4. What would change if we replaced control with shared responsibility?
5. If interdependence were our default, what decision would we make differently tomorrow?

These questions are uncomfortable on purpose. Growth usually is.

HOT TIPS for Global Organisations (Read This Carefully)

If you want your team to **actually absorb** this chapter — not just nod politely — here's how to implement it:

🔥 Tip 1: Read It Together, Not Alone

Ask teams to read this chapter **before** strategy sessions.

Connection must come *before* execution — or execution will collapse later.

🔥 Tip 2: Ban Titles for One Conversation

Run one meeting where hierarchy is paused.

No job titles. No ranks. Just humans solving problems together.

The results will surprise you.

🔥 Tip 3: Link KPIs to Impact, Not Just Output

Add one metric that measures:

- Collaboration
- Inclusion
- Shared success

What gets measured gets protected.

🔥 Tip 4: Train Leaders to Listen Before They Lead

Most leadership issues are not competence problems — they are **relational blind spots**.

Teach leaders to listen for what is *not being said*.

🔥 Tip 5: Make Interdependence a Daily Language

If your culture celebrates only individual wins, don't be shocked when silos form.

Celebrate shared wins loudly.

Make interdependence visible.

This chapter is not here to inspire you for five minutes.
It is here to **change how you see people —**
and once that changes,
everything else follows.
Interdependence is not optional.
It is how humanity survives —
and how organisations truly scale.

CHAPTER 10
The Global Language of Interdependence
IF ITCLLIGENCE FAILS, CONNECTION.
When intelligence fails, connection restores.
Key Questions
What unites people across cultures?
Why division always comes before collapse?
Why history repeats without connection?
What unites people across cultures?
Section 1 – One World, One Human Language
Whatever Separates us this brings us back together –
Interdependence Spans All Differences
Whatever separates us, this brings us back together —
because from Asia to the Americas, from boardrooms to villages…
Safety
Belonging
Dignity
Purpose • Contribution
We all share the same heart language.
Safety Belonging Dignity Purpose
4. The Interdependence Scale.
CIS8 | yourself | RARELY ~ 3 | ALWAYS)
1 I seek to understand before judging.
2 I recognize how my success impacts others.
3 I speak up when exclusion is happening.
4 I build bridges instead of camps.
5 1 One Small Action Creates Ripples.
Listen to someone you deeply disagree with,
Support a cause that does not bereft you drectly.
Replace criticism with curiosity ~ specaily at we
One world. One human language.
1 Below Neotal 3.intngthening 3.hmonity.
One world. One human language. Only interdependence speaks it.

TEAM DISCUSSION GUIDE

Interdependence in Action: A Leadership & Team Discussion Guide

How to Use This Guide

- Ideal for leadership meetings, offsites, or team development sessions
- Allow 45–60 minutes
- Psychological safety required (no blaming)

Discussion Section 1 — Awareness

1. Where do we operate in silos without realising it?
2. When pressure rises, what behaviours increase here?
3. Where do people feel unheard?

Discussion Section 2 — Responsibility

4. How does my role impact others — beyond my KPIs?
5. Where do we protect territory instead of outcomes?
6. What does shared success actually look like here?

Discussion Section 3 — Action

7. What is one behaviour we must stop tolerating?
8. What is one behaviour we must start modelling?
9. What is one experiment we will run in the next 30 days?

Closing Reflection

"Interdependence is not about being nice.

It is about being responsible — for ourselves, and for one another."

Optional Team Commitment

Each participant completes:

*One way I will take care of myself **for the team,** so the team can take care of the system **with me.***

My Notes/Take-aways

Chapter 11 — Practical Interdependence Workbook

Now that you understand interdependence globally — the only question left is:

How will you practice it personally?

This workbook is designed to help you apply interdependence across all areas of life through reflection, daily action, and measurable practice.

How to Use This Chapter

Each life area includes:

- Short story (personal or observed)
- One uncomfortable truth
- One practical action
- Reflection prompts

Living Interdependence in Daily Life

Interdependence does not ask you to change the world overnight.

It asks you to change how you show up — consistently.

It is not an ideology. It is a lived practice. A daily fluency.

A decision repeated until it becomes identity.

If I don't act, others may not.

If you don't act, others may not.

Every small choice creates ripples.
Every act of connection shapes ecosystems.
Every time we lift others, we rise.
We are all drops of water — together, we form the ocean.
So the question is no longer *"Is interdependence important?"*
The question is: How will I practice it today?

PART 1: THE 3Ls BLUEPRINT
The Framework for Practicing Interdependence

① LOVE → CONNECTION

The world does not move through power or intelligence alone.

It moves through **trust**.

And trust is built through love — not just romantic love, but *chosen care*.

Before we share language, culture, contracts, or borders, we share one thing: **the need to be seen and safe**.

Many great leaders believed force creates obedience —
but history keeps proving this:

Only love creates loyalty that lasts.

Or in simpler words, from me to you:

People don't follow titles. They follow how you make them feel.

Love also means forgiveness.

In a world place, in a messy world, full of challenges and people who came from different backgrounds, carrying different past, pains and weaknesses, we can easily get hurt by each other, sometimes intentionally, sometimes accidentally.

To practice the best in Love at INTERDEPENDENCE, we must understand that

LOVE = SACRIFICING = FORGIVENESS.

A STORY OF FORGIVENESS (LOVE)

When you love someone, you forgive them.

My father used to be violent toward my mum.

I hated him for a time — yet I still loved him.
As a child, that contradiction was very confusing.
As the years passed, I realized something painful but honest: the burden of unforgiveness was weighing *me* down.
I simply couldn't carry it anymore.
One day, I travelled all the way home from Hong Kong.
Back then, there were no express trains.
I had to connect through multiple forms of transport, passing through unfamiliar towns with bad reputations.

As it got later and the sky grew darker, my anxiety rose.
I was afraid of being kidnapped or harmed.
My mum wasn't home, so I started calling my dad, asking for help.
When he finally answered, he said only a few words:
"I'm busy. Just come back. You'll be fine."
I asked, "What are you busy with?"
He replied, "Playing poker. No time to talk."
And then he hung up.
I was shocked.
Anger, confusion, and frustration flooded me.
Are you kidding me?
How on earth do I have a dad like this?
Gambling is more important than his daughter?

For those who have read my earlier books, you may know the full story.
But the point here is this:
He was often selfish and consistently put his own interests ahead of everyone else.
That night, I didn't even have a place to sleep.
I stayed at my auntie's house, in my cousin's old room.
I didn't sleep at all, and I cried for at least an hour while all past painful memories came up to my mind. Tears were filled with sadness and anger, and I was feeling that I wasn't good enough.

The next morning, my dad called and asked me to come home.

The first instinct, of course I did not want to go, but after considering, one voice from inside of me was saying: *How long can you hide? Are you not going to meet him again? Just go; you have to face it, so be brave!*

"Yes, I need to be brave," I said to myself.

When I arrived, I saw him in the kitchen, cutting carrots.

There were a few dishes already on the table.

I was still angry.

But seeing him cutting carrots was… unbelievable.

You have to understand — this was a man who had depended on his mum and his wife to cook his entire life.

I had never seen him cook. Ever.

He is 1.72cm tall, a man who never does housework, now standing there doing something he never did…

In that moment, my heart softened a little.

He cut the carrots into small pieces because he remembered that I loved that dish, just like what my mum would always do.

That was how he remembered me.

I asked, "Did you cook these?"

He couldn't face me (still protecting his ego and to avoid the embarrassment). He stayed in the kitchen and said quietly, "Yes… maybe not very good, but I did my best."

I asked, "Can you cook?"

He replied, "No… but I'm learning."

Then I asked: "How long did it take you to cook all of these?"

He said: "About two to three hours."

I paused for a long time.

He didn't say sorry — that word never existed in his dictionary.

But his actions were his apology.

We didn't say much after that.
Yet deep inside, we were communicating without words.
I moved on, I chose to forgive and let go.

From that day on, I chose to show more compassion toward my dad.

I realized something life-changing:
The unforgiveness I carried had imprisoned me.
It stopped me from embracing a better future.
Yes, I was angry.
Yes, he made many wrong decisions.
Yes, he was irresponsible.
But when I truly understood love, I understood this:
Love means sacrifice.
Love means forgiveness.
I love my dad — despite how imperfect he is.
He is still my dad.
And the moment I chose to forgive him,
I became free.
It opens doors for the future of hope.
I said to myself: "My past does not need to become my future!"

How about you?
What are you still holding a grudge over?
Do you know that unforgiveness is the worst revenge against yourself —
and the best revenge for anyone who wants you to fail?

Daily Practical Action (LOVE)

Today: Reach out to one person outside your usual circle —
not to gain, not to ask, not to impress —
but to check in, encourage, or thank.
Connection always starts with initiative.

Reach out to someone who may have hurt you.

Tell them you have forgiven them — and see what happens.

And remember:

Forgiving does **not** mean forgetting.

Choosing to forgive means choosing freedom — giving yourself more space for the future.

2 LIVE → EXPERIENCE

To live globally is not about passports.
It is about **exposure**.
Experience stretches the soul.
Fear shrinks it.
The more we experience,
the less we judge.
The more we collaborate,
the less we isolate.

Some thinkers said, *"Travel is education."*
I say this instead:
Experience doesn't just educate you — it humbles you.

I've travelled across 20+ countries
and ever talked to people from over 190 countries.
Different accents.
Different beliefs.
Different behaviours.

Yet everywhere I went, I found the **same needs**:

- To feel safe
- To be respected
- To belong
- To live with purpose

Once you truly experience other cultures,
it becomes impossible to hate blindly.
Experience taught me this:
We are far more alike than different.

Daily Practical Action (LIVE)

👉 **This week:** Step into **one unfamiliar environment** —
a new room, a new conversation, a new culture, a new perspective.
Growth always lives just outside comfort.

③ LEARN → GROWTH

Every interaction is a classroom.
Every collaboration is a lesson.
Growth does not come from control.
It comes from **curiosity**.

Many say knowledge is power.
I say this instead:
Applied learning is freedom.

Every shipment I managed,
every negotiation I led,
every cross-border deal I witnessed
taught me something no textbook ever could:

Success scales faster when shared.

The most powerful leaders I've met were not the loudest.
They were the best learners.
And every failure — including million-dollar failed deals —
became tuition for wisdom I now carry.

Daily Practical Action (LEARN)

👉 **Each night:** Ask yourself three questions:

- What did I learn about others today?
- What did I learn about myself?
- What did I learn about connection?

Growth begins with reflection.

The Truth:

Interdependence is not cultural.

Not political.
Not religious.
It is **human**.
And once you practice it daily —
in love,
in experience,
and in learning —
you don't just become more successful.
You become **more whole**.

PART 2: SEVEN LIFE AREAS WHERE INTERDEPENDENCE LIVES OR BREAKS
This is where theory becomes lifestyle.

1. HEALTH — You Are Not Strong Alone

Do you remember the last time you were sick?

So sick that you couldn't do anything or focus on anything?

If you have to battle your health, it is impossible to build a kingdom.

Even if you won the whole kingdom, without the foundation of good health, what is the point?

Success and wealth are high-energy products.

Do you remember how successful Steve Jobs was — and still is after his death?

He could have lived such a great life, but unfortunately, he didn't have enough time to truly enjoy it.

We are not here to go to extremes — only chasing health and comfort — but we must be real and sincere:

No matter how much money you make, without health, you will suffer — and so will your family and everyone around you.

Taking care of your health is not selfish.

It is selfless and intentional.

Uncomfortable Truth:
Neglecting your health burdens those who rely on you.

Because when you keep neglecting your health, those around you suffer with you.

Action: Choose a health accountability partner.

Reflection: Who benefits when I take care of myself?

2. WEALTH — Money Is a System, Not a Trophy

SGN began with one Australian company.

Networks multiplied opportunity — not just our members, but friends' friends, and then friends' friends' friends joined us.

Have you ever thought that if you have a certain amount of money, you will finally be "wealthy"?

Wealth includes income, profit, and assets. Money itself has no value — it only has value when it is exchanged for value and service.

And value and service are meant to serve people.

I love what I heard from Myron Golden. He said something like this:

"Don't use people to serve money. Use money to serve people."

Uncomfortable Truth:

Money isolated loses meaning; money circulated creates opportunity.

Action: Map your financial interdependence network.

Reflection: Who benefits when I win?

3. SPIRITUAL LIFE — Meaning Grows in Community

Living without spiritual faith is like living with an empty bottle — without water.

If you want to live fully, spirituality is something you cannot avoid.

Have you ever thought about where you are heading after death?

Have you ever asked yourself why you exist in this world?

Have you ever discovered the purpose of your life?

These are core questions of spiritual life.

What I can say is this: I believe the rules were set clearly by God — who never intended us to be alone, but always surrounded by community.

During COVID, like many others, Luke and I felt stress and depression during lockdown.

Thankfully, our church community was there. We ran life groups online, and every week we gathered together.

In those hardest and darkest days, whenever I felt down, the people from the community lifted me up.

It gave me meaning. It gave me purpose.

Through hearing each other's stories, our faith grew stronger.

I didn't realize it at the time, but when I looked back, I saw this clearly:

When I helped others heal, I was healed at the same time.

Uncomfortable Truth:
Faith isolated becomes fragile; faith shared becomes resilient.

Action: Share one spiritual reflection or ritual this week.

Reflection: Who benefits when I act from my values?

4. FAMILY & RELATIONSHIPS — Connection Requires Courage

Family and relationships sit at the top of your life — they take up the largest portion of it.

Relationships heal when judgment stops and presence begins.

Through my childhood story, it wasn't only my mum who was the victim.

I was also the forgotten one who suffered — watching everything happen.

For years and years, I couldn't let go, until I realized I had to make a choice:

Stop judging and start understanding.

Stop living in the past and start living in the present.

I couldn't choose the beginning of my life or the family I was born into.

But I could choose forgiveness.

I could choose love.

And I could choose to create a beautiful future with my new family.

Uncomfortable Truth:

Most relationships don't break from hatred — they break from avoidance.

Action: Have one intentional conversation this week.

Reflection: Where can I choose repair instead of retreat?

5. RECREATION & JOY — Joy Is Meant to Be Shared

Joy fuels interdependence.

Collaboration grows where joy lives.

In life and career, we can easily become so busy with responsibilities and duties that we start making excuses to neglect recreation — the very place where joy lives.

The side effects?

We lose joy.

We lose creativity.

We lose our inner child.

In modern days, everyone is obsessed with personal space and **"me time."**

But the moment you involve someone in recreational activities, life lights up.

Think about a child playing alone versus playing with other children — the passion and joy are incomparable.

Every child, and every human, is naturally designed to connect.

My life lesson:
When you share stress, stress decreases.
When you share joy, joy multiplies.
(Of course, there are exceptions — especially with people who are jealous — but generally, this is the rule.)
When was the last time you did something you truly loved?
What were your most joyful memories?
I can confidently say this:
The **best moments** always involved **someone else**.

Uncomfortable Truth:
Celebrating alone is beautiful — but celebrating together is far more powerful.
Action: Invite someone into your joy (a meal, a walk, a celebration).
Reflection: What shared moment could multiply connection?

6. PERSONAL GROWTH & LEARNING — Growth Multiplied

You can learn daily and collect stories every day, but you cannot fully use or sustain knowledge…
until you share it or use it to help someone else.
Knowledge kept alone fades.
Knowledge shared compounds.
Life is a journey of learning.
Learning fuels the soul.
It gives energy to the engine.

Uncomfortable Truth:
Any tool becomes rusty if unused.
Any skill fades if unused.
Any knowledge disappears if you don't teach it.
Action: Mentor, teach, or join a mastermind.
Reflection: Who can grow because I grew?

7. PURPOSE & CONTRIBUTION —
Purpose Is Reciprocal

From babysitting neighbours' children to building global networks — purpose expanded through contribution.

The story of being fed by one neighbour was just one of many.

Almost all my neighbours and relatives fed me.

That experience shifted me — from being shy, to being grateful, to being deeply connected.

I chose to babysit their children and spend time with elderly people, even a 90-year-old granny.

These experiences built strong bonds across generations.

They also gave me the ability to connect with people of any age, speak to strangers anywhere, anytime.

I didn't realize it then, but looking back, I see this clearly:

When I chose to contribute, **the biggest gainer was me**.

It would be impossible for me to become who I am today without these experiences.

Uncomfortable Truth:
Sometimes, the person who changes your life starts as a stranger — but it only happens when you give with purpose, without expecting returns.

Action: Support one person or group meaningfully this week.

Reflection: Who benefits from my purpose — and who will next?

PART 3: DAILY FLUENCY TOOLKIT

One day at a time. One choice at a time.

Self-Check Questions

✔ Where am I lifting others?

✔ Where am I isolating myself?

✔ Where am I choosing comfort over courage?

✔ Where am I choosing love over convenience?

Daily Practice
 One Action of Giving — time, attention, resource, support
2 One Action of Listening — without interrupting or re-hearsing a reply
3 One Action of Forgiveness — someone else, or yourself
Forgiveness is not approval.
It is freedom.

PART 4: WEEKLY INTEGRATION

📌 Ask yourself:

- What relationships strengthened this week?
- Where did I choose ego over connection?
- Where did love require courage?
- What will I practice differently next week?

Growth is not linear. It is intentional.

PART 5: THE INTERDEPENDENCE MANIFESTO

We are all interconnected to each other, from the beginning, on-going and in the future. Not any single person is an isolated island of itself, just like the whole nature, nothing exists alone. Everything is interconnected. In Christianity, we are called the body of Christ, and we are one. We are all connected, and the breath of one becomes the breath of all.

We are all interdependent to each other – admit or not. We cannot live without each other. I don't know about you but I cannot imagine a day without others around. I can write books and songs, but I cannot do the baby delivery for someone. I can cook nice dishes but I cannot go and grab those meat or be the one killing any animals, if I had to, I'd rather not eat or just be the vegetarian. The day when I understand about Interdependence, I no longer feel overwhelmed anymore, because we are not meant to do everything by ourselves individually. We are meant to do all things together by using each other's gift. We are meant to serve each other. **I am me because of you and you are you because of me.**

This is not perfection. This is direction.
We Choose Interdependence

- Let love rule over hate
- Let faith rule over fear
- Let truth walk with grace
- Let service replace ego

We Become Living Proof

Strength does not require isolation.
Success does not require domination.
Humanity is not weak — it is powerful together.
Interdependence is how families endure.
How companies thrive.
How civilizations rise.
And it begins — quietly — with you.

Once again, now that you understand interdependence globally,
the only question left is personal:
How will you live it?
Not someday — today.
Lift someone.
Teach someone.
Connect someone.
Because you are only whole through others —
and together, we are unstoppable.
The choice is ours.
The responsibility is ours.
The future is ours to shape — through courage, compassion, and interdependence.

In this chapter, we practiced interdependence at a personal level — how it lives inside us, shapes our daily choices, and becomes part of who we are.

But personal fluency alone is not enough to lead teams, organisations, or systems.

To scale interdependence beyond the individual, we need structure.

—— **CHAPTER 11** ——

PRACTICAL INTERDEPENDENCE WORKBOOK

How Will You Practice Interdependence?

Now that you understand interdependence globally — the only question left is:

How will you practice it personally?

How to Use This Chapter:

 **Short story** (*personal or observed*)

 **One uncomfortable truth**

 **One practical action**

Daily Practical Action (LOVE)..
► Reach out to one person outside your usual circle — not to gain, not to ask, not to impress —
► but to check in, encourage, or thank. *Connection* always starts with initiative.

Each life area includes:
► Short story (personal or observed)
► One uncomfortable truth
► One practical action
► Reflection prompts

① LOVE → CONNECTION (LOVE) 

Reach out to one person outside **your usual circle** — not to gain, not to ask, not to impress ..

but to check in, encourage, or thank.

Part 2: THE 3Ls BLUEPRINT: *The Framework for Practicing Interdependence*

 **HEALTH** → CONNECTION

To live globally is not *about* passports. It is about exposure.

 Experience stretches the soul. Fear shrinks it.

LIVE → EXPERIENCE

To live globally *is not about* passports. It is about **exposure**.

Step into one unfamiliar environment — *new culture*.

LEARN → GROWTH

Every interaction is a classroom. Every collaboration is a lesson.

⑪ Ask yourself three questions:

⑫ what did I learn about others *today*?

⑬ what did I learn about *myself*?

⑭ what did I learn about *connection*?

Part 3: SEVEN LIFE AREAS WHERE INTERDEPENDENCE LIVES OR BREAKS

1. Health — You Are Not *Strong Alone*

2. Wealth — Money Is a System, Not a Trophy

3. Spiritual Life — *Meaning Grows in Community*

4. Family & Relationships - *Connection Requires Courage*

5. Recreation & Joy - Joy Is Meant to Be Shared

6. Personal Growth & Learning - *Growth Multiplied*

7. Purpose & Contribution - *Purpose Is Reciprocal*

④ DAILY FLUENCY TOOLKIT

● Where am I lifting others?

● Where am I isolating myself?

● Where am I choosing comfort *oar urage*'

Part 3: THE INTERDEPENDENCE MANIFESTO

 In this chapter, we practiced interdependence at a personal level — how it lives inside us, shapes

INTERDEPENDENCE *by Kristy Guo*

My Notes/Take-aways

Chapter 12 — The Interdependence Framework™

Interdependence in Action: The 3 Ls and the 5 Ps**

In Chapter 11, we explored the 3 Ls as a personal practice.

In this chapter, I will show you how the same principles operate at a **leadership and system level** — inside teams, organisations, cultures, and communities.

Let me be very honest with you.
Most philosophies sound beautiful.
Most systems sound intelligent.
Very few actually **work together**.
That's why many people feel inspired on Sunday…
and exhausted again by Monday.
So in this chapter, I want to do something different.
I want to combine **how we feel** with **how we function**.
Because leadership without heart becomes cold.
And heart without structure becomes chaos.
That's where **Interdependence** lives.

The leadership philosophy & system translation: The 3 Ls — Love, Live, Learn

Before we talk about systems, KPIs, or performance, we must talk about being human.

Because no system ever failed due to lack of intelligence —it failed because of **broken relationships**.

I call this the **3 Ls**.

Not because it sounds nice (though it does),

but because every healthy human system already follows it — consciously or not.

LOVE — Connection Before Performance

Let me be clear.

Love is not romance.

Love is not weakness.

Love is not hugging everyone at work (please don't).

Love is **consideration**.

It is the decision to see people as humans *before* seeing them as roles.

In leadership, love looks like:

- Listening before reacting
- Respecting before correcting
- Creating safety before demanding results

People don't leave companies — they leave **disconnection**.

And yes, love belongs in leadership.

If that sentence makes you uncomfortable, that's usually a sign it's needed.

Love is the invisible infrastructure of every high-performing system.

LIVE — Responsibility in Action

Love without action is just a nice speech.

To **live** means:

- To show up
- To take responsibility
- To embody what you say you believe

Culture is not what's written on the wall.

Culture is what people do when nobody is watching.

In leadership:

- Your behaviour trains more than your words
- Your consistency builds more trust than your titles

You don't lead by telling people what to do.
You lead by living what's right.
Values that are not lived are just decorations.

LEARN — Adaptation Is Survival

Here is a truth many successful people struggle with:
The faster you succeed,
the harder it becomes to stay humble.
But systems that stop learning… stop surviving.
Learning means:

- Listening even when it hurts
- Accepting feedback even when your ego disagrees
- Updating your thinking when reality changes

In life and leadership:

- Curiosity beats control
- Humility beats arrogance
- Learning beats knowing

The fastest way to fail is to believe you already know.

So that's the **philosophy**.

But philosophy alone won't scale a team, a company, or a legacy.

That's why we need the system.

The System: The 5 Ps of Interdependence

If the 3 Ls are **how interdependence feels,**
the 5 Ps are **how interdependence works.**
This is where leaders stop saying:
"People are the problem,"
and start asking:

"How do we design better systems for people?"

1 PRESENCE — Are You Actually Here?

You can't build connection if you're physically present but mentally absent.

Presence means:

- Listening without planning your reply
- Being available, not just visible
- Paying attention to what's not being said

In teams:

- Presence reduces conflict
- Presence builds trust
- Presence creates loyalty

You cannot lead people you are not present with.

2 PURPOSE — Why Are We Together?

People don't commit to tasks.
They commit to **meaning**.

Purpose answers:

- Why does this matter?
- Who does this serve?
- What are we building together?

Without purpose:

- Teams burn out
- Sales feels empty
- Success feels lonely

With purpose:

- Effort becomes meaningful
- Sacrifice becomes voluntary
- Growth becomes sustainable

Purpose turns work into contribution.

③ POSITIONING — Know Your Role in the System

This is where many leaders struggle.
Interdependence does not mean:
"I do everything."
It means:
"I know my role, and I respect yours."
Positioning is about:

- Clear responsibilities
- Healthy boundaries
- Mutual respect

In a system:

- Everyone matters
- No one does everything
- No role is insignificant

Confusion creates conflict.
Clarity creates collaboration.

④ PARTICIPATION — Interdependence Requires Action

You cannot outsource responsibility and still expect belonging.
Participation means:

- Contributing, not just consuming
- Speaking up, not sitting back
- Engaging, not withdrawing

Whether in a family, team, or organisation:

- Participation builds ownership
- Ownership builds pride
- Pride builds excellence

Interdependence only works when everyone plays their part.

5 PROSPERITY — Growth That Lifts Everyone

This is my favourite one.

Prosperity is not just money.

It's:

- Emotional health
- Relationship depth
- Sustainable success

True prosperity means:

- When the system grows, people grow
- When people grow, the system grows

This is where competition transforms into collaboration.

Hoarding creates loss.

Giving creates abundance.

How the 3 Ls and 5 Ps Work Together

Let me simplify this for you.

Philosophy (Heart)	System (Structure)
Love	Presence + Purpose
Live	Positioning + Participation
Learn	Prosperity (continuous growth)

Or as I like to say:

The 3 Ls shape **who we are**.

The 5 Ps shape **how we operate**.

When both exist, interdependence becomes natural — not forced.

A Final Thought (From My Heart to Yours)

You don't need to become someone else to master interdependence.

You don't need to be softer or tougher.
You don't need to be perfect.
You only need to be **intentional**.
When you:

- Love with awareness
- Live with responsibility
- Learn with humility

And design systems with:

- Presence
- Purpose
- Positioning
- Participation
- Prosperity

You don't just build success.
You build **people**, **relationships**, and **legacy**.
And that, my friend,
is leadership that lasts.

— **CHAPTER 12** —

THE INTERDEPENDENCE FRAMEWORK™

Interdependence in Action: The 3 Ls and the 5 Ps

In Chapter 11, we explored the 3 Ls as a personal practice. In this chapter, I will show you how the same principles operate at a leadership and **system level**—inside teams, organizations, cultures, and communities.

Philosophy + Systems = Results

Love fuels Connection, Live fuels Responsibility. Learn fuels Adaptation.

The 3 Ls — Love, Live, Learn

LOVE—Connection *Before Performance*

- **Listening** *before reacting.*
- **Respecting** *before correcting.*
- **Creating safety before** demanding results.

LIVE—Responsibility *in Action*

- Your **behavior** trains more than your words.
- Your **consistency** builds trust than your titles.

 *Love fuels Connection, Live fuels Responsibility, Learn fuels Adaptation.*

The 5 Ps — How Interdependence Works

PRESENCE
Are You Actually Here?

- Listening without planning your reply.
- Being available, not just visible.

PURPOSE
Why Are We Together?

- Why does this matter?
- Why does this serve?
- What are we building *together*?

POSITIONING
Know Your Role in the System

- Clear responsibilities
- Healthy boundaries.
- Mutual respect

L♡VE + How Interdependence + The 5 Ps

① PRESENCE	**②** PURPOSE	**③** POSITIONING	**④** PARTICIPATION
Are You Actually Here?	Why Are We Together?	Know Your Role	Growth That Lifts *Everyone*
 Listening *without planning your reply.*  Being available, *not just visible.*	▸ Who does this matter? ▸ Who does this serve? ▸ What are we building together?	Clear responsibilities Healthy boundaries Mutual respect	Emotional health. Relationship depth Sustainable success.

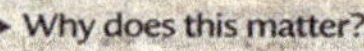

When both exist, Interdependence *becomes natural—not forced.*

A Final Thought (*From My Heart to Yours*) 

INTERDEPENDENCE *by Kristy Guo*

My Notes/Take-aways

Continue the Journey

If this book resonated with you, it may be because you, too, have a story worth sharing.
The Signature Influencer Author Program invites leaders and changemakers to contribute their experiences to future volumes.

🌐 kristyguo.com/signature-influencer-author-program

Join a Global Community of Thought Leaders
Leadership isn't about standing above others — it's about standing with them.

Here, you can:
- Share your leadership journey to inspire others
- Connect with purpose-driven leaders worldwide
- Leave a meaningful legacy through your story

Your voice matters. Your story has value.
📩 Email cuilanguo@outlook.com to express your interest.
Legacy begins not with perfection, but with courage.

Stay connected:

Connect with Kristy by scanning the code above

Connect with SGN by scanning the code above

GIFT -Complementary E-Book Downloading

You can get the Free Download For The Secret Success Guidebook:

Through this link: https://signaturegln.marketing/giveaway

Author's BIO

Kristy Guo (Cuilan Guo) is a global connector, leadership mentor, and the founder of one of the world's fastest-growing international logistics networks. But more than her titles, it is her lived experience across cultures, industries, and human stories that shaped the ideas in this book.

Born into complexity and raised in an environment where survival depended on unseen support systems, Kristy learned early that no one truly succeeds alone. From a childhood shaped by scarcity and separation, to working across borders and continents, she witnessed firsthand how people, communities, and nations rise—or fall—based on how well they understand connection.

Over the past two decades, Kristy has worked with leaders, founders, and CEOs across more than 90 countries, guiding them through growth, failure, reinvention, and leadership challenges. Through global trade, cross-cultural negotiations, and thousands of conversations with people from up to 190 countries of different backgrounds, beliefs, and values, one truth became undeniable: interdependence is not a theory—it is a law of life.

Her work spans business, leadership, family, faith, and community. She has built global platforms that unite people who would otherwise remain strangers, helped leaders scale organisations while preserving humanity, and turned competition into collaboration across cultures. English is not her first language, yet she has authored multiple books—each rooted in real life rather than perfection.

Kristy's philosophy is shaped not only by professional success, but by motherhood, marriage, faith, failure, forgiveness, and daily choices. She believes leadership begins at home, that strength multiplies when shared, and that love, humility, and responsibility are not weaknesses—but power.

Interdependence was written not to teach superiority, but to restore perspective. Not to sell a system, but to offer a language the world has forgotten.

Kristy lives in beautiful city -Melbourne, Australia with her husband and children and continues her work helping individuals, families, leaders, and communities build meaningful, connected lives—one relationship at a time.

Contact ***Kristy Guo:*** www.kristyguo.com

www.signaturegln.com
LinkedIn (Cuilan Guo): https://www.linkedin.com/in/cuilan-kristy-guo-1776b5182

SGN Annual Event 2023 – Ho Chi Minh, Vietnam
60+ multinational global leaders wearing
Vietnamese Traditional Costumes.
Not every attendee was featured on the photo

SGN Annual Event 2024 – CEBU, Philippines
90+ multinational global leaders
Not every attendee was featured on the photo

SGN Annual Event 2024 – Xiamen, China
100+ multinational global leaders
Not every attendee was featured on the photo

SGN Annual Event 2025- Bangkok, Thailand
120+ multinational global leaders
Not every attendee was featured on the photo

*"Interconnection is a default, interdependence
is a decision."*

Kristy Guo

www.ingramcontent.com/pod-product-compliance
Lightning Source LLC
Chambersburg PA
CBHW051453050726
47593CB00005B/2044